Ethics for Social Care in Ireland:
Philosophy and Practice

Ethics for Social Care in Ireland: Philosophy and Practice

Manus Charleton

GILL & MACMILLAN

Gill & Macmillan Ltd
Hume Avenue
Park West
Dublin 12
with associated companies throughout the world
www.gillmacmillan.ie

© Manus Charleton 2007

978 07171 4257 6

Print origination by Carrigboy Typesetting Services
Index compiled by Cover to Cover

The paper used in this book is made from the wood pulp of managed forests. For every tree felled, at least one tree is planted, thereby renewing natural resources.

A CIP catalogue record is available for this book from the British Library.

For my wife, Barbara, and daughters
Oonagh, Medb and Muireann

Contents

Acknowledgments

I would like to thank the students of applied social care with whom I have discussed ethics over the years. Their experience and knowledge have been particularly helpful. Sarah Banks's books on ethics in social work have been a particular source of help. I would also like to thank my colleagues on the Applied Social Care course at Sligo Institute of Technology for their support. My family has been particularly supportive and encouraging. Also to my family and friends many thanks for your perspectives in the lively discussions we continue to have. They have been of great benefit. In particular, I would like to thank Gerard McCarthy.

Preface

What are we to make of ethics now in Ireland? In the 1990s and early 2000s it became public knowledge that some people were failing to observe basic standards. Examples included the physical and sexual abuse of children where some of this abuse was carried out by members of the clergy and occurred in institutions established for the care of children. Other examples included banking and business scandals, tax evasion by some prominent politicians, political corruption and, in 2006, wrongdoing by gardaí in performing their duties. While the number of people involved has been small, the effect on our understanding of people's relation to ethics has been deep and widespread, and in particular on our notion of Ireland as a caring society. It is because of both the devastating nature of the failures and the fact that those involved represented institutions and organisations which have leading and responsible roles in society that faith in ethics has been understandably shaken. Loss of trust in others has been one understandable effect, scepticism for ethics another.

Unethical conduct in banking, business, politics and law enforcement may not seem to relate directly to social care, but it does indirectly in contributing to a climate in which disregard for the consequences of behaviour toward others is seen as acceptable. Unethical behaviour in these areas also affects social care when it results in a loss of money to the state, money which the government could use for social care services. On the wider front, ethical standards and practices are also an issue affecting care. For example, we still live in a world in which millions suffer from malnutrition and preventable diseases and have a short life expectancy. This marks a failure by governments and by the international community to provide for the value of human rights.

One response to the setbacks ethics has received is to look again at values to see what they offer and why they are important. This book has been prompted in part by that need in the context of teaching ethics to students of social care. What do values mean for both the theory and practice of social care? For example, how should the social care value of responding to people's need for well-being be understood, especially in cases where circumstances are complicated? Understanding what values mean can help provide clarity in making care decisions and formulating plans. More generally, there is the question of what social justice should mean for social policy.

There have been calls for a public debate on the values which should inform Irish society. Concern has been expressed that in a more prosperous Ireland, people have become less inclined to practise the value of looking out for others. Economic growth is clearly important as a moral enterprise since it provides the good of prosperity for more people. Prosperity provides more opportunity for people to choose the kind of life they want. However, there is concern about the emphasis that is placed on growing the economy as an end in itself, with less attention given to ensuring that the growth is sustainable in social and environmental terms and in terms of making people happier. A value that has assumed ever greater importance for people is the improvment of their own material position through acquiring more money for cars, houses, holidays, etc. This is linked to a decline in the value of community as well as public support for providing services for more vulnerable members, such as older people, those experiencing poverty or those with a disability, support which a wealthier Ireland is now better able to afford. There is a saying that 'a society's level of civilisation can be measured by how well it treats its weakest members.' On this scale, those who are concerned about social care are asking how high Irish society rates.

Philosophers have provided some understanding for the gap between people's declared values and their actual behaviour. Spinoza, whose ideas are examined in Chapter 7, points to the power of causes to affect our behaviour to an extent that is beyond our control. As a result, people can find themselves doing the opposite to what they know to be good. From experience, we know our behaviour can often fall short of standards we expect of ourselves. Montaigne referred to the gap when he wrote 'that is the way humans proceed' (2003: 1119). In one meaning *proceed* suggests a certain resignation at human failings, but in another sense it suggests that we need moral standards, and indeed ideals, as directions for how we should live, even though we may not always be following the directions. It suggests how much worse off we would be if we didn't *proceed* in their light, however inadequate our efforts to live up to them, for then we might feel we could do anything we like without regard for the effect of our behaviour on ourselves and others. *Proceed* suggests we can develop a closer relationship between our behaviour and standards and ideals.

Some sense of ethics is central to how we literally *proceed* in our daily life. Ethics is not something we engage with only when a moral issue arises for us and then leave aside – it is part of our prevailing outlook. We have what Taylor calls a 'moral orientation' or framework (1989: 99). It characterises our responses. We use it to evaluate our way through situations and issues, but it is not always clear to us that our responses contain values. This is because values are so closely bound up with how we engage with our experiences. For Iris Murdoch, our values show in 'what we see things as, what we let, or make, ourselves think about.' Things, people, situations we encounter every day have *moral colour*. This may be black or white, but usually it is one of a large number of subtle shades of grey (1992: 215;

265). This makes it important to know what is of value, and why we and society generally can try to have a life according to what is of value.

We use moral language all the time, often investing it with emotional conviction. However, what people mean by *ethical* and *moral* and related terms can sometimes come across as assertion which may, or may not, be well-founded. Whether done intentionally or not, moral language can even be used to manipulate others where it disguises self-interest. For example, we can notice when people and governments behave with double standards. One benefit of understanding values is that it will enable us to be more critically aware of the way moral language is used and what it means.

Asked what he thought of Western civilisation, Ghandi famously said that 'it would be a good idea'. In other words, he appreciated the values on which Western civilisation is based but recognised that they were not being adhered to in practice. This book is about some of those values. It is based on the belief that the better we understand these values, the more likely it is that this will contribute to living up to them in practice. The book specifically aims to enable people who work in social care to have confidence in knowing that there is a body of theory about values that can be considered to inform, support and provide justification for their work in caring for others.

REFERENCES

Murdoch, I. (1992) *Metaphysics as a Guide to Morals*, Chatto & Windus.
Taylor, C. (1989) *Sources of the Self: The Making of the Modern Identity*, Cambridge University Press.
Montaigne, M. de (2003) *The Complete Essays*, Penguin Classics.

1
Introduction

OVERALL AIM

The aim is to introduce ethics as a subject of study in relation to providing social care.

LEARNING OBJECTIVES

At the end of this chapter you should be able to:

- Connect with the book's overall aims.
- Distinguish ethics as a subject from its relation to religion, law and politics.
- Relate ethics to a professional code for guiding best practice.
- Identify particular care values, principles and practices explored in the book.
- Begin to engage with ethics as a subject involving exploration of ideas about values and principles and their relation to practice.

AIMS OF THE BOOK

- Develop a deeper and more informed understanding of the ethical purpose and practice of social care through understanding the values and principles that guide it.
- Provide a means of contributing to ethical decision-making, especially in cases for best social care practice.
- Critically evaluate social care conditions and issues in the light of knowledge and understanding of values and principles.

In this chapter we will look first at ethics as a subject in relation to social care before looking ahead at the values and related practices and how they are covered.

APPLIED PHILOSOPHY

As a subject, ethics is a branch of philosophy. Philosophers try to provide reasons why certain things should be considered moral values and principles. In practice, ethics also relates to the behaviour of people in society and to the moral norms and standards they follow. The approach to ethics for social care taken in this book is to bring both aspects together. Values and principles as understood by philosophers are related to the practices and issues that arise in providing care. Both are compared and contrasted in considering examples.

Ethics and *morality* are used interchangeably. At the same time, you will find that *morality* tends to be used to refer to people's values and principles and to norms and issues in society. *Ethics* tends to be used in a broader sense to refer to the understanding of values and principles and their place in people's lives and in society.

Ethics and Religion

Ethics has always been central to human living. There have always been requirements or expectancies about how to behave. Traditionally these have come from the community or culture, which in turn located the source of the requirements in a belief in the existence of an all-powerful God. Historically, ethics is associated with religious belief. This is still very much the case for billions of people who believe in a particular religion such as Christianity, Islam and Judaism. They get their ethics from belief in the teaching of their religion about the behaviour God expects from them if they are to lead good lives. A central element of religious morality is care for people in need. Before the state became involved in providing care, it was provided through voluntary, charitable work, mainly by people who saw it as one practical way of living their religious belief. Such work remains a part of care services today.

However, ethics is not confined to religion. Outside religious belief, people still need to know how they should act and what they should do. They need to know where the authority lies that holds them accountable for their actions, or if there is no such authority apart from law. Also, in a democratic society there is a separation between church and state. This means that the state cannot endorse the moral teachings of a particular religion, or religions, on the basis that they are required because of religious belief.

As a subject within philosophy, ethics is different from religion. It does not accept views on faith. As far as possible, it is based on rational thought. Ethics tries to establish the kind of behaviour appropriate for people through rational thinking. As we shall see, moral requirements from the main ethical theories have care for others as a central element.

Ethics and Law: The Overlap

Ethical and legal requirements often overlap, particularly for behaviour that directly harms others. The law supports some ethical requirements by making non-compliance with them a punishable offence. For example, while it is morally wrong to harm another person physically, the law supports this in the case of domestic violence, by enabling the spouse who is a victim to obtain a court order barring the spouse who has been violent from access to the family home. The law reinforces many ethical requirements by imposing a penalty for non-compliance in the interests of the protection of citizens and for the good of society. One way of putting this is to see law as exerting an external force to make us comply with certain minimum acceptable moral standards for living with others in society.

Another feature of the overlap is legal provision of services, and of rights, on the basis that they are ethically required. For example, a particular issue in relation to social care is legal entitlement for people with disabilities to special needs services as a right. We will look at this issue in Chapter 5.

At the same time, it's not the law's job to make us morally good. While ethics overlaps with law, it is distinct from it.

Ways in Which Ethics Is Distinct from Law

Freedom of Choice

In the interests of providing for personal freedom in a democracy, there has to be a large sphere of activity in which it is a matter for the individual to choose how to behave without any legal restriction. People are free, for example, to end their marriage commitment if they so choose and to seek a divorce (under divorce legislation). This point about personal freedom, morals and the law was made in the Wolfenden Committee's report in Britain as far back as 1957 in recommending that homosexuality be decriminalised. The report stated, 'There must remain a realm of private morality and immorality which is, in brief and crude terms, not the law's business' (Hart 1962: 14–15).

Self-regulation

Ethical behaviour can be characterised as complying with requirements where we have a certain freedom to comply or not. This highlights self-regulation as an important feature at the heart of ethics. Ethics is about regulating our own behaviour in particular ways, either because we want to or feel we have to even if we don't want to, rather than from fear of having to pay some penalty if we don't and are found out. For example, we don't have to be compassionate, speak out against injustice or always tell the truth. These are matters for us.

Usually people behave in ethical ways because they believe they are *the right ways* to behave; they don't do so simply because they feel they have to conform or because the law requires them. Whether a law existed or not, they would still try to behave ethically. They see it as important to do the right thing for its own sake.

Ethical Basis of Law

If law is to command respect and obedience, it has to be based on what citizens in general consider ethical. For example, because the former apartheid laws in South Africa which treated black people less favourably than white people were seen as morally wrong, people felt justified in disobeying them and campaigning for their abolition. That a particular law might be considered unethical serves to highlight how law needs to be based on the understanding of what is ethical if it is to be acceptable. It highlights how ethics can be considered a deeper court of appeal than law.

Ethics and Politics

Ethical Basis for Politics: Theory and Practice

In theory the purpose of politics is to provide for *the good* of all citizens. This makes ethics a natural precursor to political activity. Politicians are often criticised for not allowing values and principles to influence their policies and decisions sufficiently. One reason for this is that political parties need to win and retain power if they are to have influence. This has led to an emphasis in politics on providing for the demands of particular groups in society whose support politicians seek in order to have power. Politicians will sometimes admit that certain groups which already do well from society have too much influence over public policy and decisions. Such groups are often referred to as 'vested interests' because of the keen interest they take in how decisions are made in order to gain from them. There are many such groups. The main groups are the employer associations, professional associations and trade unions as well as particular industries, such as construction, and services, such as banking. A consequence of the influence of vested interests on political decisions is that the public good of those who have social care needs may not be catered for as well as it deserves to be. At the same time, there is a number of organisations and groups who represent the interests of those in need of care, such as the Children's Rights Alliance and Age Action Ireland, as well as agencies set up by the government, such as the Combat Poverty Agency and the National Disability Authority.

Politics and State Welfare

The idea that the state should provide people with welfare arose from acceptance of the ethical argument that it was wrong to leave people who were unable to provide for their own needs to rely on charity. As a result, state provision of measures such as old age pensions and disability benefit were introduced. Utilitarian ethics, known by *the greatest happiness principle*, which was developed in the late nineteenth century, is said to have had a significant influence on Britain becoming a welfare state. We will look at this theory in Chapter 6.

Politicians make the laws, and legal provision of care services is the strongest way of ensuring they are actually provided. Each year in Ireland the Finance Act gives legal force to the measures in the budget. From a care perspective the main measures in the budget are the amount of money by which benefits are increased. Conditions for eligibility for benefit may also be improved or made more restrictive. Also, the net overall effect of budgets on people's living standards can be judged in terms of social justice, i.e. in terms of the people who benefit the most from the measures introduced, whether they are the middle- and high-income earners or low earners and those on social welfare. We will look at ideas about social justice in Chapter 11.

Politics and the Vision of a Good Society

At a broader level, political parties have particular ideas and beliefs about what the social good means. These ideas owe their origin in part to the ideas of political philosophers. Chapter 10 explores social contract ethics and looks at the ethical ideas associated with different types of political theories regarding what providing for the social good means.

Ethics and Professional Codes of Conduct

Professions have a code of conduct by which their members are required to abide in practising their profession. Codes vary and can have a number of different purposes. One purpose is to provide a service ideal of values and aspirations for professionals to try to fulfil. Another is to set down the requirement for professionals to be trustworthy in their relations with clients (also called 'service users' in social care). Respect for the client's liberty and independence is central. This is to help ensure that all service providers are clear that any exploitation of the client is professional misconduct. Abiding by a code is particularly important for those who work in social care because many clients are vulnerable.

Professional ethics can be regarded as 'an intensification of ordinary ethics', with particular reference to 'interpersonal trust' (Kohen cited in Banks 2004: 61). Both ordinary ethics and professional ethics can be seen ultimately to derive their requirements from ethical ideas about values and principles. Banks points out that while many of the ethical issues belong specifically within the nature of the profession and the professional's role, they nevertheless draw from moral philosophy.

As she puts it, 'it is important to be able to locate professional ethics in the broader field of philosophical ethics and to use the insights and arguments of philosophy to illuminate and develop our thinking' (Banks 2004: 74).

Some of the values and principles explored in the book have particular relevance to a code of conduct for those who work in social care, notably the value of respect.

PREVIEW OF CARE VALUES, PRINCIPLES AND RELATED PRACTICES

Well-being

This value is related to care practices such as:

- Developing a client's capacity for self-determination as far as possible in relation to his/her circumstances.
- Providing practical assistance through support services to enable the client to achieve well-being.
- Providing for social inclusion and integration of clients and client groups within their family and community.

The source for the value is explored in Aristotle's virtue ethics.

Respect and Care

Respect is related to practices such as:

- Informing and consulting clients on matters relevant to their care.
- Maintaining confidentiality subject to care requirements.
- Providing equality of treatment.

Care is related to:

- Providing care on the basis of a duty to care and on the basis that the extent to which the duty is met is the extent to which people and society can be considered good.
- Assisting a client's self-development.

The source for the values of respect and care is explored in Kant's morality of universal principles.

Human Rights

Human rights are related to:

- Providing services to enable clients to have a basic acceptable standard of living and to have equality of treatment comparable to everyone else where they have special needs.
- Supporting the legal provision of certain rights to strengthen the requirement to provide for them in practice.

Sources for human rights are explored in natural law theory and in international agreements and Irish law.

The Greatest Happiness Principle

- This principle is related to reducing hardship in society through practical assistance to ensure everyone's happiness is catered for as much as possible.

Its source is located in Bentham and Mill's utilitarian principle of 'the greatest happiness of the greatest number'.

Empathy

Empathy is related to:

- Helping clients as a result of recognising understandable difficulties they face in coping with their freedom.
- Removing or reducing restrictions to the freedom that clients face from conditions such as poverty, incapacity or old age.
- Relating to clients on the understanding that they may have limited responsibility for their circumstances and actions.

Sartre's idea of personal freedom as a difficult challenge is explored as one reason why empathy is a value – another reason is practical restriction, e.g. poverty. Spinoza's idea that free will does not exist because behaviour is determined by causes is explored in particular as a reason for empathy.

Acceptance of Difference

This value is related to:

- Accepting all people regardless of moral difference resulting from cultural background or viewpoint.
- Promoting the integration of diverse cultural groups in society.
- Recognising that there are some limits to practices considered morally acceptable.

A source is seen to lie in ideas of relativism deriving from Moore's view that good cannot be defined and from standard arguments for moral relativism.

Social Well-being

Social well-being is related to:

- Supporting the practice of the virtues, such as compassion, restraint and courage, as necessary for the well-being of all in society.
- Promoting concern and care for others as a central social practice necessary for the well-being of society.

Reasons for the importance of social well-being are explored in MacIntyre's virtue ethics.

Social Contract Ethics

Social contract ethics is related to:

- Influencing the direction for social policy on the basis of an informed view of what constitutes the social good.
- Seeking the good of clients on the basis of an informed view.

Sources for the value of social contract ethics are derived from Hobbes's and Rousseau's idea of the social contract.

Social Justice

This value is related to:

- Influencing the direction for social policy on the basis of an informed view of what social justice means.

- Seeking justice for clients for whom it can be argued that they are being treated unjustly compared to the rest of society on the basis of an informed view.

Sources for the meaning of social justices are looked at in Aristotle's view of it as the right proportion, Rawls's view of it as fairness and Nozick's view of it as entitlement to holdings obtained voluntarily.

GUIDE TO CHAPTER MATERIAL

The introduction to each chapter dealing with a particular value looks at its meaning in the context of examples of practical issues and problems which those who work in social care encounter. The body of the chapter then looks in some detail at the reasons which provide the basis for the value and at the relation between the value and social care. In each chapter there are also questions for consideration and discussion or an exercise or case study to provide a means of applying the value to practice.

At the end of each chapter there is a section on critical evaluation of the value for those interested in exploring the philosophical aspects in more depth. One of the reasons for including this section is to show that there are limitations (as well as strengths) to our understanding of values. In general, this is one reason which can help care workers to understand why they work in an environment where values are not rationally compelling for everyone, where people differ in their moral views and where there can be moral uncertainty.

You will find that values are connected and often arise together as different facets of the same ethical requirement. As you go through the book you can then begin to look at a particular issue from the perspective of different values to see how informative they are for guiding the appropriate ethical response.

SUGGESTED APPROACH

You could look on your exploration of the values in a similar way to how Wittgenstein is said to have looked upon philosophy, i.e. taking you on different journeys in order to find your way about a strange town. On many of these journeys you pass the same place or close to it. No one journey is necessarily more important than another. Eventually you get to know your own way about (Drury, 'Wittgenstein': 5).

Questions for Consideration and Discussion: Legal Responsibility of Children and Parents

Do you think that twelve is the appropriate age at which a child may be considered to have full understanding of its actions in order to be held criminally responsible for offences and that for serious offences, such as murder and sexual assault, a child from age ten may be considered responsible?

Do you think the law should remain which enables judges to require parents whose neglect to care for their children is considered a contributory factor in their children's offences to pay compensation for damage their children cause where they have the means to do so?

In forming your viewpoint, consider the care implications, then identify the values and principles on which your viewpoint is based.

REVIEW

Ethics is a distinct subject which tries to establish values and principles to guide behaviour. In practice for social care it is closely connected with law and politics. Political decisions and law-making are the main processes through which services (and their funding) come to be provided for those who are in need of care. Ethical requirements are used as justification for the need for improvements in the provision of services. Ethical requirements are also central in formulating a code of practice for those working in social care.

FURTHER READING

Banks, S. (2004) *Ethics, Accountability and the Social Professions*, Palgrave Macmillan.

Banks, S. (2006) *Ethics and Values in Social Work*, 3rd ed., Palgrave Macmillan ('Preface', 'Introduction' and Chapter 4 on 'Professionalism and Codes of Ethics').

Banks, S. and Nohr, K. (eds.) (2003) *Teaching Practical Ethics for the Social Professions*, FESET (European Social Educator Training/Formation d'Educateurs Sociaux Européens). (See www.feset.org)

Bateman, N. (2000) *Advocacy Skills for Health and Social Care Professionals*, Jessica Kingsley (Chapter 3, 'Ethical Principles for Effective Advocacy').

Benn, P. (1998) *Ethics*, UCL Press ('Preface').

Honderich, T. (ed.)(2005) *Oxford Companion to Philosophy*, 2nd ed., Oxford University Press (contains useful entries on ethics).

Norman, R. (1998) *The Moral Philosophers: An Introduction to Ethics*, 2nd ed.,
    Oxford University Press ('Introduction: Ethics and its History').
Roth, J. (ed.) (1995) *International Encyclopaedia of Ethics*, Fitzroy Dearborn (a very
    useful synopsis of many aspects of ethics).
Thompson, M. (2003) *Teach Yourself Ethics*, Hodder Headline ('Introduction').

JOURNALS

Journal of Social Work Values and Ethics (see http://www.socialworker.com/jswve)
Ethics and Social Welfare

SOME INTERNET SOURCES

Irish Social Care Gateway (provides up-to-date information on applied social
studies and Irish society)
http://staffweb.itsligo.ie/gateway/

Irish Association of Social Workers
www.iasw.ie (see especially for their code of ethics)

Comhairle
(National Agency for information, advice and advocacy on social services)
www.comhairle.ie

Ethics Updates (useful introductory site for students, particularly on the theoretical
aspect of ethics)
http://ethics.acusd.edu/

Ethics in Practice
www.stpt.usf.edu/hhl/eip

FESET (European Social Educator Training/Formation d'Educateurs Sociaux Européens)
www.feset.org

Manus Charleton's site
www.itsligo.ie/staff/mcharleton

REFERENCES

Banks, S. (2004) *Ethics, Accountability and the Social Professions*, Palgrave
    Macmillan.
Banks, S. (2006) *Ethics and Values in Social Work*, 3rd ed., Palgrave Macmillan.
Drury, M. 'Wittgenstein', *Context*, No. 3, UCD Philosophy Society.
Hart, H. (1968) *Law, Liberty and Morality*, Oxford University Press.

2
Social Care Values and Principles

OVERALL AIM

To explore the meaning of care values and principles and relate their meaning to the work of meeting social care needs.

LEARNING OBJECTIVES

At the end of this chapter you should be able to:

- Explain the meaning of values and principles.
- Understand care for both oneself and others as a basic way in which the world is experienced.
- Explain what Taylor means by the value of having 'a full life' and relate it to the work of providing social care.
- Describe the social care advocate's role as bridging the gap between what is the case and what should be the case in service provision for clients.
- Explain how ethical considerations form part of making best practice decisions in casework.

VALUES AND PRINCIPLES

When we use a phrase such as 'you should do this' or 'you ought to do this' in an ethical sense, we do so on the basis of a value we hold. For example, 'you should take it easy' or 'you ought to get out more' imply our belief in the value of a person's well-being. Also, when we say of a person that 'he has a right' to something, such as special needs education, it is on the basis of the value of human rights. When we refer to certain basic values in this way, we usually do so expecting they will be values for others. We regard values as the kind of things that should generally have influence in guiding behaviour. This is because values point out the direction for understanding behaviour that is good or right. From this comes the commonly used term 'moral compass'. We might speak of people (usually others, or society, not ourselves!) as having lost their 'moral compass' when we consider they have gone off the track morally.

Values highlight the worth that certain actions and practices have which bear them out. For example, well-being highlights the worth of a whole range of actions and practices relating to physical, emotional and social health. It is because values refer to things that have worth that people want to try and live by them and practise them. They enable us to have a good life.

> They [moral values] refer to things we consider worth cherishing and realising in our lives. Since judgments of worth are based on reasons, values are things we have good reasons to cherish, which in our well-considered view deserve our allegiance and ought to form part of the good life.
>
> Parekh 2000: 127

Besides being about values, ethics is also about principles. Principles are also expressions of certain actions and practices that are considered to be right. An example of an ethical principle often cited is 'always treat other people as you would like them to treat you'. Some ethics, notably Kant's, place emphasis on the existence of principles we should follow whether we value them or not. In ethics for social care, we can look on principles as the kind of things that guide the practical expression of care values. For example, respect for people is one of the main social care values, and one way of expressing it is through the principle of enabling clients to make their own informed choices.

CARE AS A BASIC ORIENTATION AND VALUE

Care itself is a core orientation we have which we value. Furrow refers to two interrelated senses of care. One, which draws from Heidegger's philosophy, identifies care as the basic way in which people come to give meaning and value to their experience (Furrow 2005: 133). It is because we *care* about our life, health, family and friends and about material prosperity that these things and relationships come to have meaning and value for us. Caring is what human beings do. In Heidegger's terms, care describes our very being in the world. People who do not care will usually have mental health problems, perhaps chronic depression or despair. They are seen as in need of care so that they can then begin to care again about their lives. Underlying the things we value, we value our capacity to care. We can say that care and value are in a reciprocal relationship: care enables us to have things in our lives that we value, and we value care because we have things we value on account of it.

We get our values, then, from the things we care about. However, some people care about (and value) things that are not morally good. This may be their power to take unfair advantage. This may be their skill as a thief! This is why we need to explore values to know which ones are good. Also, while care for others is a good value, not all care is ethically good care. For example, it will not be good if it is provided without respect for the client. Thus care of others as a value has itself to be qualified by further values in order to be good.

Not everything we care about and value would seem to relate to ethics, strictly speaking. For example, a person may care about and value his car, and this would seem to be of no moral significance. But if we look at ethics in the broadest sense, then it relates to the things to which we give our energy and attention, to how important or unimportant they are for us. For example, if a person was to value his car or his socialising to the neglect of his children, then this would bring his relation to these things into the ethical sphere. This is not to devalue either having a car or socialising. As we will see in looking at well-being as a value, things we naturally desire are morally good, but we look to ethics for guidance on the values that are of most importance.

Values of most ethical importance are often referred to as *core values*. However, even among core values, decisions are sometimes required which accord priority to one over the other. This is often the case in care work. An example would be to accord more value to a client's well-being in protecting him/her from self-harm than to the value of respect for his/her independence. Thus we also need ethics to help us have clarity on the relative importance of values in particular cases.

The second sense of care identifies it as a practical virtue through which we 'nurture and preserve what has value' (Furrow 2005: 133). In this sense, care relates to preserving and nurturing the things and relationships we value, such as helping others where we can.

Care and Being Human: Ancient Latin Fable

Once when *Care* was crossing a river, she saw some clay; she thoughtfully took up a piece and began to shape it. While she was meditating on what she had made, Jupiter came by. *Care* asked him to give it spirit, and this he gladly granted. But when she wanted her name to be bestowed upon it, he forbade this, and demanded that it be given his name instead. While *Care* and Jupiter were disputing, Earth arose and desired that her own name be conferred on the creature, since she had furnished it with part of her body. They asked Saturn to be their arbiter, and he made the following decision, which seemed a just one: 'Since you, Jupiter, have given its spirit, you shall receive that spirit at its death; and since you, Earth, have given its body, you shall receive its body. But since Care first shaped this creature, she shall possess it as long as it lives. And because there is now a dispute among you as to its name, let it be called *homo*, for it is made out of *humus* (earth).

(cited Heidegger 1967: 242)

From earliest times, care has been a central theme in the recorded stories of the peoples of the world. Such stories revolve around the kind of things and relationships that people see as having meaning for them and what they value. One of the things the stories show is the value people place on providing care through practical assistance to others who are in need. The above ancient fable captures the fundamental place of care in human life.

In summary, care is a basic human orientation which we exercise under the guidance of values.

CARE FOR ONESELF AND CARE FOR OTHERS: THE TWO DIMENSIONS

In general, people's understanding of ethics is that it has to do with a person's, or with a society's, relation to others. In particular, it is seen to be about not causing harm to others and looking after people in need who are unable to help themselves. This view of caring about, and caring for, others does identify the main dimension of ethics. But there is another dimension, which is closely related to it. This is the dimension of caring for oneself. To care for ourselves means more than looking after our own physical and emotional needs in so far as we can. More specifically, in an ethical sense it means having self-knowledge in order to recognise certain things as having worth or value. We are then in a position to try to live our life according to what we value by giving attention and energy to the activities and practices that express those values.

The practice of an ethics of caring for oneself in accordance with values has been called 'the art of living'. Like any art, it can be practised well or badly. It relates to how we manage or conduct ourselves in a whole range of everyday situations, some of which are demanding, according to the things we recognise as having value.

Care of the self in this sense has long been recognised as central to ethics. Before Socrates was put to death in ancient Athens (for going against the norms of his society in trying to get people to think about how they should live), his friends asked him how he would like them to care for his wife and children. He said his wish was that they should care for themselves. He was not advising them to be selfish or to do nothing for his family. He was expressing the view that the best basis from which to care for others is to have a developed sense of care of oneself.

Socrates' last wish, prompted by his concern for his family, is that his friends care for themselves; only in that way will they be able to care for his children or, for that matter, for anyone else. The care of the self, as I have argued, precedes, or perhaps constitutes, the care of others.

Nehamas 2000: 167

A particular reason for developing ourselves through self-care is to avoid a situation where we may be caring for others partly to compensate for neglecting ourselves. Our care for a client may then be more about ourselves and our needs than for his/her sake.

Overall Value of a Full Life

Taylor points out that even if morality is seen only in terms of how we should relate to others, this still leaves another big dimension of life in which we need to make value choices. It relates to making value choices to have 'a rich meaningful life' or 'a full life' for ourselves, one that is suited to us as an individual with particular talents and interests. He further points out that many people make choices around this value in terms of providing themselves with an 'ordinary life'. By this he means in particular seeking fulfilment in relationships with family, friends, work and personal interests. It is particularly in this area where we seek fulfilment through these activities that the two dimensions of caring for oneself and for others show up as interrelated (Taylor 2000: 14–15).

Value of a Full Life and Social Care

From a social care perspective, the value we place in having a full life for ourselves through our choices highlights the particular value of enabling clients to make choices regarding their own lives, as far as possible, and to depend less on care services. By enabling clients to do this, a care worker is empowering them. It may be to perform some basic activity or to live independently with support, or to make their own choices, for example, in how they would like to spend their time.

The value we place on having a full life highlights the value of providing care services. This is because we do not all have the same opportunities to have a life based on our value choices. People who need social care can be seen as experiencing practical restrictions in having a full life for themselves, restrictions which can be removed or alleviated through the provision of services. A simple example where a service can remove such a restriction would be providing transport for older people in isolated rural areas to and from a centre for social activities.

ADVOCACY AND CARE

Advocacy as a particular aspect of social care is underpinned by the moral case for improvements in care. It is based on the value of helping others to have their needs met by speaking on their behalf to the relevant service providers. The service providers are usually the staff in state or voluntary agencies that make the decisions on service provision.

The need for advocacy is based on the recognition that different sections and groups in a democratic society have varying degrees of influence over public policy in having their interests satisfied. Some lose out in having their needs met because they have little or no influence over public policy. Advocacy is the means for them to have a voice in achieving their needs. It is seen as particularly necessary for members of certain groups, such as older people, those with a disability or the homeless, who may have limited ability or opportunity to speak on their own behalf and are therefore vulnerable to having their needs neglected. At the heart of social care advocacy lie values such as human rights and respect. Social fairness or justice are other broader ethical ideas that arise within advocacy in social care.

Advocates try to bridge the gap between what should happen to meet care needs and what happens in practice. It is the gap between the level and quality of care provided through public policy and the needs of service users. This attempt to bring about change or improvement in practice is the moral thrust that runs through their work. In effect, the advocate draws from values when s/he argues on behalf of a client whose needs are not being provided for that those needs *should be* provided for.

APPLICATION OF VALUES AND PRINCIPLES TO CASES

A background in understanding ethical values and principles is not just informative for guiding social care provision, but helpful for ethical reasoning in particular care cases. Ethical reasoning is often necessary due to the complexity of cases. For example, in the particular case of an older person who is unable to cope on his/her own, there can be a clash between supporting the values of both independent living, where s/he insists on it, and ensuring his/her health and safety. Also, difficult issues can arise in some cases where, for example, the rights of parents to rear their children can be in conflict with their children's right to safety and protection. In such cases, a decision may have to be made about whether to leave the children in the care of their parents or relatives or to obtain a court order to take them into the care of the state. Such issues can take the form of a dilemma. This is where we are faced with having to choose between alternatives, each of which is a hard choice because it contains elements that are not desirable but are unavoidable. Dilemmas may involve a care team in making a risk assessment before taking a decision whether to trust people whose behaviour is a cause of legitimate concern.

Dilemmas highlight the fact that, apart from distinguishing right from wrong, ethics relates to the more challenging questions of distinguishing degrees of right from lesser degrees of right. Making ethical decisions often requires the ability to make distinctions between competing choices and to justify one choice over another.

In social care casework there is a growing accumulation of knowledge and experience and there are established procedures for best practice in particular types of cases. However, each client's circumstances will be unique and this can make a case complex. Also, apart from new variations of familiar factors, complexity can arise from the emergence of new and unexpected ones. This means that in assessing a client's circumstances, there has to be a certain openness to according weight to particular factors and, as a result, to the balance between them in making the best decision. Central to this process is concern for the client's good – understood as his/her best interest. Factors to do with the good of others related to the client and the good of society can also come into consideration. In short, making good decisions involves being able to reason morally on the basis of knowledge and understanding of values and principles.

Ethics requires us to think carefully with an open and questioning mind. As Banks points out, it is not possible or desirable to produce an ethics rulebook. Instead, critical thinking and reflection are required (2006: 9). Philosophy provides the tools for this thinking and reflection.

CASE STUDY 2.1

Home Support, Independence and Care

Mary is a 75-year-old woman who lives alone. She suffers from arthritis and is beginning to show signs of short-term memory loss and neglect of personal hygiene. Mary has been cared for by her daughter, who visits her three times a week. However, her daughter has made it known that she needs to scale back her visits to one day a week in the interests of looking after her own family. She also believes her mother would be best cared for in a public nursing home. However, Mary is adamant that she will not move into a nursing home. Mary is also on painkillers for her arthritis, but was advised to reduce their intake after a fall, as the sedation was felt to be a factor. Mary has informed her social worker that she intends to take an overdose of sedatives if she believes she will have to move. An assessment of Mary's care needs three months ago showed that she should be provided with daily home help for a significant number of hours. However, given the resources available to them, the HSE have said that they cannot provide the service for the amount of hours required. They said that even if they were to make an exception, it could lead to a reduction in services for others.

Consider:

1. The moral issues the case raises.
2. Your response to those issues in relation to care values and practices.

Exercise 2.1

From your knowledge and experience of social care, describe a case in which ethical issues arose in the provision of services to meet needs that had been identified for a client. Relate your response to the ethical issues to your understanding so far of social care. (Note: If you draw from a case known to you rather than a hypothetical case, ensure you refer to the issues only and not to identifiable people. Confidentiality is an important ethical principle looked at in Chapter 4.)

REVIEW

We live in the world in a basic way by caring about ourselves and our relationships. Values and principles highlight aspects of living considered of worth, such as respect for people. In particular, they guide the care of those who have needs.

FURTHER READING

Banks, S. (2006) *Ethics and Values in Social Work*, 3rd ed., Palgrave Macmillan (read especially Chapter 1, 'Ethical Issues in Social Work', and Chapter 7 'Ethical Problems and Dilemmas in Practice').

REFERENCES

Furrow, D. (2005) *Ethics*, Continuum.
Heidegger, M. (1967) *Being and Time*, Oxford: Blackwell.
Nehamas, A. (2000) *The Art of Living: Socratic Reflections from Plato to Foucault*, University of California Press.
Parekh, B. (2000) *Rethinking Multiculturalism, Cultural Diversity and Political Theory*, Palgrave Macmillan.
Taylor, C. (1989) *Sources of the Self: The Making of the Modern Identity*, Cambridge University Press.

3
Well-being

OVERALL AIM

To explore Aristotle's virtue theory for the understanding it offers in meeting people's needs for well-being.

LEARNING OBJECTIVES

At the end of this chapter you should be able to:

- Give Aristotle's account of the relationship between satisfying desires and achieving overall well-being, understood as flourishing.
- Explain what he means by virtue and why he thinks the practice of virtues provides for well-being.
- Explain why he thinks our own well-being is bound up with the well-being of others.
- Understand that poverty and bad luck can restrict a person's chances of doing well.
- Describe the relationship between Aristotle's ethics and care practices in meeting needs for basic support, social inclusion and client self-empowerment.
- Explain why behaving according to particular virtues is beneficial for clients and for guiding care providers in complying with best practice.

INTRODUCTION

There are many aspects to well-being, and different client groups have different well-being needs. The following are some examples.

- A family may have a need for support services where parents have difficulty coping because of poverty or lack of parenting skill.
- Elderly people in care and people with disabilities have needs for fulfilling activities.

- Clients in residential care have a need to exercise choice in their lives as much as possible, e.g. over the food they want and leisure activities.
- Clients who are homeless have needs for long-term secure accommodation.
- Clients capable of independent living have a need for support services.

ETHICS AND VIRTUE

Aristotle's theory is known for being the prime example of ethics based on virtues. It is the practice of virtues, he claims, that will lead to well-being. So what are virtues? Virtues are qualities that a person has and puts into practice. Aristotle calls them dispositions to behave in particular ways. There are many virtues – they include honesty, loyalty, courage and compassion, etc. We will look at virtues more closely later on in the chapter. It will help to see what Aristotle is getting at to keep them in mind from the start.

DESIRE TO FLOURISH

Desire to Satisfy Basic Needs

For Aristotle, everybody desires to flourish. (For an image of flourishing, think of a plant doing really well and transpose that image onto a person!) The desire to flourish is a central desire of human beings. Even though some people are not flourishing, maybe because of restrictive living conditions or because of behaving in misguided ways harmful to themselves and others, they still have a desire to flourish. It is what we all desire most.

The desire to flourish is evident first of all from the fact that we have natural desires to satisfy our physical and social needs. Much of our behaviour is directed toward achieving these desires. For example, we desire food, education, a job, friends, etc. Such things that we naturally desire are good, and they are the first step on the way to understanding moral goodness as the desire to flourish. In Aristotle's terms, in seeking to achieve our desires, we are seeking to achieve *our ends*. This makes behaviour *teleological*, i.e. always directed toward achieving some end or goal.

Aristotle points out that when we examine our desires, we see that we usually desire something for the sake of something else. We desire food for the sake of satisfying hunger or for the pleasure of taste; we desire education for the sake of knowledge and qualifications (or, of course, for the love of learning!); we desire a job for the sake of money and the satisfaction of exercising our abilities; we desire money for the sake of all the things we can buy with it; and we desire friends for the sake of the enjoyment and fulfilment that comes from close relations with others. Desire, therefore, consists of wanting various means for various ends.

One Overall Desire: To Flourish

However, Aristotle claims that human desire amounts to more than the satisfaction of particular desires. He would not see the person who had everything he wanted in terms of being able to satisfy all his particular desires as having no other desire left unfulfilled. There is something still missing, and this is the achievement of the desire to feel we are flourishing in our life. That is, we would still not be happy, and to be happy is what we desire most. (We will look more closely at the relationship between flourishing and happiness shortly.) He says that we do not *experience* our desires as *only* a series of means to ends and nothing more. If we attend closely to our desires, we can notice that in seeking to satisfy all of *our particular desires*, we also feel ourselves to be seeking, in and through them, to satisfy *one overall desire*. This one overall desire is the desire to flourish.

Also, he believes particular desires, if they are to make sense, have to be leading to some overall fulfilment. Otherwise the only meaning and value they have lies in the amount of satisfaction we can get from them. This would then be all we could expect for our well-being, but human beings have a sense that they are capable of achieving more. So he maintains that the things we desire are always desired *for the sake of* something else, with one major exception, and that is the desire to flourish. This is the one desire that is desired for its own sake.

Another way of putting it is to say that there is one good we desire which is good in and of itself. He calls it a self-sufficient good. By self-sufficient he means a good 'which on its own footing tends to make life desirable and lacking in nothing' (Aristotle 1955: 37). For him, this is flourishing. It is living 'the good life'. Aristotle can be credited with being the author of this now much-used phrase, though somehow I don't think it is always used to mean what Aristotle meant by it!

How are we to understand the good life or flourishing? Also, how are we to go about achieving it? The Greek word Aristotle uses is *eudemonia*. *Eudemonia* is sometimes translated as *happiness*. *Happiness* today means different things to different people. For Aristotle, it had one particular meaning. We often associate happiness with the good feeling we get from a particular experience, such as success in exams or the birth of our child. As Aristotle understood it, such good feelings are related to happiness since they are the achievement of natural desires. However, occasional good feelings from the achievement of desires do not, for him, make up the full meaning of happiness.

Also, people often associate happiness with a feeling of contentment. However, while happiness could be said to include an element of contentment, it is not quite like it since contentment suggests a passive state of being. For Aristotle, happiness has the more active meaning of a person *living well or faring well* in general or in relation to all aspects of their life (29). It is for these reasons that the English words *flourishing* or *thriving* are said to be closest to the meaning of *eudemonia* as Aristotle intended. Perhaps our understanding of the ordinary phrase 'doing well' comes close to Aristotle's meaning now for its sense of well-being through activity.

But what should a person do in order to do well? Aristotle's answer is that we should use our reason to regulate our feelings and desires.

DEFINING FUNCTION OF REASON

Desires are the main factor giving rise to how we behave. We desire something and, as a result, our behaviour is directed toward achieving it. Our feelings also give rise to our behaviour. For example, when we feel upset or frustrated, we will behave in some way as a reaction to such feelings. Perhaps more noticeable for us than our desires or feelings in influencing how we behave are the courses of action open to us from the situation we are in. But how we respond in practice to these courses of action, i.e. which one we opt for, depends on the kind and degree of desire or feeling we have toward them.

However, we are not solely under the influence of our desires and feelings. This is because we also have reason to guide our choice. We can reason about our desires and feelings in order to make the best choice of how to respond to them. For Aristotle, reason is central. Why is reason so important? It is because reasoning is something only humans can do. It distinguishes us from plant and animal life. It is our defining function. For Aristotle, man is a rational animal. We all have a function by virtue of our nature as human beings and that function is to reason well about how we should behave (37–9). He argues that if we fulfil our defining function, we are behaving as we ought to behave and will flourish. No more can be expected of us. We are living the life fit for a human being whose nature is made up of both desire and reason.

In identifying our human function with reasoning, Aristotle distinguishes it from a job function, or social function, or the function of exercising a particular talent. These functions are good. It is good that we perform these functions as well as we can. They contribute to human flourishing. For example, it is good that a builder builds a house as well as he can; it is good that a parent performs the role of being a parent well; and it is good that a musician plays well. For the individuals concerned, these are examples of their human potential being realised. These are good things, and we can admire the results (39).

However, Aristotle's key point is that neither exercising a particular job, social function or talent will on *its own* fulfil our human desire for flourishing. Human flourishing comes about essentially through reasoning about our desires and feelings in the context of the particular circumstances that have aroused them – and then making a good decision as to our response. For example, what is important is how the builder handles being let down by workers who don't turn up; it is how the parent handles the moody assertiveness of their adolescent son or daughter as they undergo the transition from childhood to adulthood; it is how the musician handles an inattentive audience or bad review; it is a whole host of other feelings and desires that they, or any person, experiences in the course of any day.

Ethics, for Aristotle, is particularly about the nitty-gritty, day-to-day challenges to our response. For example, on any ordinary evening you may feel tired after a long day and want to relax and watch TV. Yet you may also feel like obliging a friend who phones and wants you to go out to a disco. In addition, you may have a niggling feeling that you should start writing an essay which is due shortly. Then there's your mother, whom you promised to phone, but you have been putting off phoning her because you are afraid she will have something to say to you about your behaviour that you don't want to hear. What Aristotle is saying is that you should become as clear as you can in your mind about your feelings in response to this situation, *with a view to making the rational decision which will enable you to flourish best in the circumstances*. The right rational decision here is difficult since you are pulled in different directions, which is often the case with moral decision-making. And Aristotle is not going to tell you what your right rational decision should be. He does offer general guidelines, as we shall see, but essentially what you decide will depend on your own judgment about what will best enable you to flourish in the particular circumstances.

In this way, ethics is about making good judgments around our desires and feelings in the context of practical matters that arouse them. We need to deliberate well about what is the best thing to do in the light of how we feel.

DOCTRINE OF THE MEAN

How do we reason well about our desires and feelings to make the right decisions? Aristotle's answer is his famous doctrine of the mean. This doctrine provides guidelines for making a decision. But what is the *mean*? The mean is the midpoint between the two extremes of excess and deficiency of the particular desire or feeling. Excess is over-reacting; deficiency is under-responding. He uses the role of diet in relation to health as an example. Health is adversely affected by eating and drinking either too much or too little. It is adversely affected by excess or deficiency. But it is produced, maintained and improved by choosing to take the right quantity (58).

He calls the mean between excess and deficiency a virtue: 'virtue discovers the mean and deliberately chooses it' (66). Here we meet again the word *virtue*, which we said at the beginning is central to Aristotle's understanding of ethics. In choosing the mean as the midpoint between the excess and deficiency of a particular desire or feeling, we are choosing the virtuous response. We will look next at some examples.

With regard to desire for food and drink, the midpoint, or mean, as the virtuous response is moderation. It is precisely through eating and drinking moderately in relation to our desires for food and drink that we can act best toward having good health. Moderation is also a virtue in responding to the desire for any physical pleasure. Aristotle is sometimes misrepresented as having the view that we should repress our physical desires for pleasure because they conflict with the rational side of our nature. For him it is a matter of *managing* our desires in our best interest. He claims moderation contributes toward enabling a person to flourish by keeping an edge to his appetite and preventing it from becoming dulled from either disinterest or overindulgences (58). Moreover, it is up to each person to decide where *moderation* lies for them in their circumstances; it is not a question of having to accept someone else's view of what moderation should mean. Aristotle vests authority and responsibility with each individual person for deciding on where virtue as the mean lies in relation to their particular needs. One way of describing moderation as a virtue is to say that it lies between extremes of avoiding being 'a slave to our passion' on the one hand and being 'a cold fish', or passionless, on the other. So for Aristotle, a capacity to enjoy physical pleasure comes best from practising the virtue of moderation. (If true, it's not a bad incentive for being virtuous!)

Further examples of virtue as the mean between extremes of excess and deficiency include the following.

Patience

When we feel it hard to maintain hope or expectancy, then patience is the midpoint between the excess of annoyance and the deficiency of being disheartened.

Courage

When we feel challenged, courage is the rational way to respond as the midpoint between the excess of recklessness and the deficiency of fear or timidity.

Assertiveness

When we feel unsure of our self-worth or self-esteem, then Aristotle would no doubt identify with the modern-day quality known as assertiveness as the rational response. Assertiveness is the midpoint between the excess of aggression and the deficiency of submissiveness. It is emphasised today as a communication skill.

Honesty (Truthfulness)

This arises from the way a person handles the feeling of concern about the consequences for him/her and others if certain information is disclosed. Excessive concern may lead to apprehension and fear, resulting in telling a lie or concealing or withholding the truth. A deficiency of concern may result in indifference to the effect of knowing the truth for well-being, resulting in not saying anything or not admitting something to ourselves. Honesty avoids the excess of acting from fear and the deficiency of acting from indifference or convenience. It also avoids the excess of desiring to succeed by misrepresenting the reality. The challenge we face in being honest or truthful arises in circumstances where the truth is awkward or hurts.

Self-restraint

When we feel frustrated, then restraint is the midpoint between lashing out and being indifferent to the cause of our frustration. Restraint is a much-needed social virtue. Many bad actions result from failure to control frustration through restraint, e.g. domestic violence, drunkenness, greed, road rage, verbal abuse or making hurtful comments.

Compassion

Compassion is feeling with others in their difficulty or plight. It can be understood as the midpoint between the deficiency of indifference to the suffering of others and the excess of being self-indulgent in allowing our emotion to flow on other people's behalf. Excess could also lead to overpowering a client with care, which would not be good for the client. An example of compassion being exercised in public policy is where the Minister of Justice grants permission for an asylum seeker who has been judged not to meet the legal requirements to remain in the country on humanitarian grounds.

Due Anger

When we feel angry about some injustice done to us or to others, then, for Aristotle, due anger is the right response (63). It is the midpoint between losing our temper (excess) and being indifferent or not bothered (deficiency). Due anger is a powerful motive for social justice, especially where the lack of justice is causing suffering, as in famine and abuse of human rights.

Justice

Justice can be understood as people's entitlement as the midpoint between the deficiency of not getting it and the excess of receiving more than they deserve. For Aristotle, a socially unjust society is one in which there is excessive wealth alongside the deficiency of poverty.

ACTION AS WELL AS THOUGHT

Of course, it's not enough to reason well and make rational decisions as to the virtuous response without doing anything. Ethics expresses itself in actions based on good decisions: 'It is not enough to *know* about goodness; we must endeavour to possess and use it, and in some way to see to it that we become good' (309). Aristotle calls the virtues, such as those listed above, the 'practical virtues'. This is because they show themselves in actions; they constitute what he calls 'practical wisdom' (67).

BAD FEELINGS

Not every desire or feeling allows us to choose the mean as the virtuous response. Some desires or feelings are bad in themselves; it is not possible to relate to them by choosing their mean in order to respond to them in a good way. Instead we simply have to try to avoid having such feelings at all. They include feelings of hatred, malice and envy. Aristotle admits he can't prove why they are wrong. He simply says they are self-evidently wrong (67).

However, it is easy to agree with him. We learn from experience that living a life in which we have these feelings will not lead to our own flourishing. For example, hatred eats us up emotionally, making it impossible to feel good. Envy takes our attention and energy away from making ourselves happy through its focus on the person we envy.

VIRTUE AS RATIONAL MANAGEMENT OF FEELING AND DESIRE

It is not so much a matter of applying reason to desire or feeling where they are two distinct aspects of our response. In practice, both are interfused. We respond emotionally in a way that can be rational or irrational. It is a matter of trying to ensure our feelings are appropriate to the situation whereby we don't overreact to something minor and underreact to something serious (Norman 1998: 38).

At the same time, we sometimes do need to exercise rational control in a distinctive way. We need to step back from strong emotions that have been aroused in us to gain rational control of them. We need to rein in our emotions in order to respond appropriately. The phrase 'blinded by emotion' is one Aristotle would well understand; indeed, our recognition of this state derives from his ethics. Being 'blinded by emotion' is to behave without the influence of rational control. Following the mean avoids the negative effects of acting on strong feelings without thought of the consequences for us or for others. One saying that captures Aristotle's ethics is when we say of ourselves that 'I let my feelings get the better of me.' Aristotle's doctrine of the mean has given rise to a number of sayings still much used today to point out appropriate behaviour. These include:

- 'The happy medium.'
- 'The golden mean.'
- 'The right proportion.'
- 'The well-balanced decision.'

VIRTUE AS POWER

As the mean, a virtue is not a safe middle course of action between responding too strongly or too weakly. It is not a compromise in which something is lost. The original meaning of *virtue* is *power* or *excellence*, and that is how Aristotle understood it. The Greek word for virtues which Aristotle used is *arête*, and it means *excellences*. The present-day term *self-empowerment* is perhaps close to the benefit Aristotle saw in practising the virtues. This term highlights the fact that it is up to each individual to achieve well-being for himself/herself (and to be helped to do so, as in social care) by making good or virtuous decisions about how to relate to his feelings and desires in any circumstances.

In order not to misunderstand Aristotle it is important to point out that while the mean *is* the virtue, there is no mean *of* virtue (66–7). In other words, it is admirable to have an excess of virtue. People who have virtue to a high degree are described as having *heroic virtues*. Nelson Mandela, for example, would be said to have practised the virtues of courage and justice to a heroic level.

Also, being virtuous does not mean missing out on a good life for the sake of some more worthy moral ideal. It is precisely that course that increases a person's power of flourishing. Aristotle also makes clear that a virtuous life is meant to be satisfying or fulfilling in a pleasurable sense (42). Virtues provide a particular source of pleasure. Thus a person who finds s/he is not happy while trying to be virtuous may need to reconsider whether s/he is choosing the mean accurately to provide him/her with the best disposition to have toward his/her desires and feelings in particular circumstances.

OUR OWN WELL-BEING INCLUDES WELL-BEING OF OTHERS

So far we have been looking at Aristotle's understanding of how an individual person should flourish. However, the fact that, as we have seen, flourishing is a self-sufficient good does not mean that we seek our own flourishing in isolation from others. There is a close relationship between a person's own flourishing and that of other people. The reason for this is that people have an essential need for each other's company: 'Man is a social animal, and the need for company is in his blood' (227). Our social nature is evident to Aristotle from the natural existence of family, friendships and the state as a community: 'By *self-sufficient* is meant not what is sufficient for oneself living the life of a solitary but includes parents, wife and children, friends and fellow-citizens in general. For man is a social animal' (37).

From our social nature comes natural feelings and desires for others to do well. Thus, for society as a whole to have well-being, its members need to practise virtues that provide for the well-being of others, such as for people with disabilities, who have desires which they cannot realise for themselves without help.

In practice, having a social nature means that in making good decisions about our own flourishing in how we respond to our desires and feelings, we have to include the effects of our decisions on the flourishing of others. There is always a social context to be taken into account. Otherwise a person's own flourishing will in some way be diminished. At the same time, Aristotle does not suggest that relations with others should have to restrict our flourishing. Both aspects come into consideration for the individual in judging behaviour appropriate to flourishing in any set of particular circumstances. Here again it is a matter of getting the balance right.

Friendship

In Aristotle's time and culture, friendship was rated highly as a value and he emphasises its role in providing social well-being. He says, 'It is one of the things which life can least afford to be without. No one would choose a friendless existence on condition of having all the other good things in the world' (227). Friendship has many good things to offer. One is that it enables us to learn more about ourselves and our options from engaging with the views of others who have had different experiences to us and whose understanding can vary from ours. Alternatively, their understanding may support ours when we have doubts. Friendship broadens our horizon, particularly in relation to intimate matters of concern to us. From friends we can get a different perspective on a problem which can release us from entrapment in our view (if it is holding us back) and contribute to providing us with a more balanced outlook to enable us to flourish. Friends can help us see and judge better our good in particular situations. 'Trusting the guidance of a friend and allowing one's feelings to be engaged with that other person's life and choices, one learns to see aspects of the world that one had previously missed' (Nussbaum 1990: 44).

Because of incapacity, or other reasons, some people who require care may not have opportunities to develop friends. Thus, it is a particularly good thing for care workers to provide opportunities for clients to develop friends where they desire them. The benefits of friendship also come from the love that family members have for each other. This is one reason why family support services are important.

PRACTICAL IMPEDIMENTS TO FLOURISHING

Aristotle recognises that a person's material circumstances have a crucial bearing on his chances of flourishing through the practice of virtues. If he lacks material goods, his activity will be impeded because he will have to devote too much time and attention in trying to meet his basic needs. For the same reason, a person needs to be free of bad luck (222). While an adequate level of material prosperity and good fortune cannot themselves provide happiness, they are necessary preconditions for it. He is also well aware of how harsh fate can be and how vulnerable a person is. In particular, if a person experiences terrible bad luck, his prospect of flourishing will either be seriously diminished or even destroyed (45).

In his clear recognition of how poverty and bad luck can restrict well-being, Aristotle has laid the foundation for the view that good actions include those that provide practical assistance. Again, the root reason for helping others lies in our social nature, through which our own good is bound up with the good of others. Therefore society is the poorer if some of its members are not doing as well as they could be for want of assistance.

DIFFICULTY FINDING THE MEAN

Finding the right or virtuous response in all circumstances is not easy. As the mean between extremes, virtue is a particular point on a scale. This makes it likely we will miss that mark. There are many ways in which the mean can be missed, but there is only one way in which it is found (73). Aristotle likens finding the mean to the archer hitting the bull's eye on the target (66).

He accepts he is not giving clear-cut guidelines. They are not possible, and we can understand why when we consider that feelings and desires are subjective states that belong to individuals. No two people are exactly the same, either in their emotional states or in experiencing circumstances in exactly the same way. Therefore the choice of the mean that expresses the virtue for one person is not necessarily the same choice for another person in the same situation. On a daily basis, each person finds themselves in many different situations unique to them requiring a specific appropriate response. Thus he says he is providing only 'a rough outline' (27). It is, then, very much up to each person to work out for himself/ herself how s/he should behave in order to flourish.

HELPFUL ROLE OF HABIT

The desires and feelings we have are often the same ones that have arisen from being in similar situations before. This enables us to develop virtue as habit. Habits are a way of making it easy to behave in accordance with the mean for recurring feelings that arise from similar situations we encounter. They save us from having to think what our virtuous response should be on each occasion. Good habits help to confirm a person in virtue as a settled disposition (56). 'Moral virtue is a habit of making the right choice of conduct' (173).

Habits enable a relatively smooth continuity of flourishing behaviour. The common understanding of ethics as related to developing good habits comes from Aristotle.

DEVELOPING CHARACTER

By acting in accordance with virtues as a matter of habit, a person develops a good character as distinct from personality. Virtues are the marks of good character: 'By *goodness* I mean goodness of moral character' (65). In the end, it is from having a good character that a person gets a sense of flourishing.

SOCIAL CARE AND ARISTOTLE'S VALUE OF WELL-BEING

Client Self-empowerment

Looking back at the elements of Aristotle's ethics, the central element relating to social care is that it is in the nature of human beings to have a desire to flourish. In order to flourish, each person is required to think about what is appropriate for his own good within the general guidelines of the doctrine of the mean. Responsibility and challenge are given to each person to make decisions in his/her own best interest to flourish. Aristotle's ethics can be seen, therefore, to underpin the values of individual empowerment and self-determination. Clients in need of care have their capacity to exercise their power limited by their circumstances, such as disability, age, living conditions and addictions. Aristotle's ethics, then, can be taken to support clients exercising their own power in so far as possible.

In practice, providing for client self-empowerment and independence can sometimes be difficult. The following are three types of circumstances that give rise to difficulty:

1. Where there is a shortfall between the desires of the client and the care measures which the agency can supply in needed support.

2. Where clients have varying degrees of learning challenge, difficult decisions can arise with regard to both supporting their choices and ensuring their protection.
3. Where there is opposition between the agency's view of appropriate care for, say, a teenage client whose relationship with parents has broken down and the views of his/her parents.

Practical Assistance

At a basic level, to provide for client well-being means providing protection against harm and neglect. Aristotle also makes clear that certain material conditions are necessary for people to flourish. Lack of material requirements and bad luck can seriously restrict a person's capacity to flourish. This underlies the view that it is morally good to assist clients through providing them with practical support to enable them to flourish as well as possible. This may have to do with some material or social need, such as housing or a specialised service for a particular disability.

Social Inclusion

Central to Aristotle's ethics is the recognition that an individual's capacity to flourish is intimately bound up with the flourishing of everybody else in society, arising from the social nature of being human. Thus, well-being of the community as a whole is diminished to the extent that some of its members experience obstacles to their full participation. This underlies the care role of providing for the social inclusion of individuals and groups who are excluded or marginalised from family, friendship or the wider community, such as the homeless, refugees or migrant workers. In particular, the major good that comes from friendship highlights the value of helping clients cope with isolation and loneliness. Older people living alone and people with significant disabilities are particularly vulnerable to being deprived of the good that comes from having close ties to others.

Provides for a Full Life

Related to empowerment, practical assistance and social inclusion is the value of leading a full life in which people can realise their potential to flourish. We have mentioned this value already in the Introduction. For Aristotle, leading a full life includes being able to exercise our particular talents and abilities as far as possible – this particularly supports care practices for those who have a disability.

Allows for Emotion

As we have seen, feelings and desires or, more generally, our emotions enter into good or virtuous decisions when they are included as the midpoint. However, in another sense our emotions are involved in having a good or right response. The way in which we first respond to another person or situation is partly emotional, and Aristotle sees this as a vital element in having a fully human response. We respond with shades of such emotions as affection or concern, and they inform the appropriate good response. Along with reason, they contribute to giving us moral knowledge. Martha Nussbaum sees Aristotle as saying that if we don't cultivate our emotional responses and go by reason too much, we can lack moral perception (1990: 78). This point about the role of emotion in giving us appropriate moral knowledge is particularly important for the traditional social care core value of empathy.

Allows for Circumstances

A significant feature of Aristotle's ethics of relevance to social care is that it is not dogmatic. Ethics arises for people in their capacity to deal with circumstances and situations as well as they can in accordance with their nature – made up of both reason and emotion. How we should respond depends on the particular circumstances of the situation that calls for our response. While the doctrine of the mean provides a general guideline, it is always under the influence of the particular circumstances. This absence of a prescriptive element, i.e. laying down the law for how everyone should behave, is characteristic of virtue ethics. A prescriptive element is, however, central to duty ethics associated with Kant, which we will examine in Chapter 4. In particular, in making a moral decision on appropriate care for a client, virtue ethics enables care workers both to recognise and take account of such factors as:

- Client circumstances.
- Pressures a client experiences.
- Client character.

Virtues and Social Care Work

Finally, Aristotle's understanding of virtues, in particular the virtues of compassion, due anger and patience can be seen to inform the work of policy-makers, managers and those who deliver and deal directly with clients in providing for their well-being. Clients, too, by practising the virtues can contribute to their own well-being. Part of social care work is assisting clients to recognise how they may need to behave with, for example, courage or patience in the interests of their own well-being.

Aristotle's Psychological Insight

A notable feature of Aristotle's ethics is his recognition of the importance of human psychology to behaviour long before *psychology* emerged as a specific human science. He did so by pointing out the powerful role played by human desire in causing behaviour. In addition, he recognised that management of desire is essential for the benefit of both the individual and society. He also pointed out that regulation of desire is something we all have to learn. This remains an essential part of the moral guidance parents give their children and, where necessary, can feature in the care guidance given to clients.

NOTE ON THE INFLUENCE OF ARISTOTLE'S ETHICS

Aristotle's ethics has had a huge influence. This is partly because his ideas became incorporated into Christian ethics. They also influenced ethics in the Islamic tradition. This has meant that his theory has influenced many billions over two millennia. In particular, he provided a basis for the understanding and teaching of traditional moral values such as honesty, compassion, moderation and justice, which are as important today as in his time. In Chapter 11 we will look at his understanding of social justice, which has also proved relevant to the present day.

Exercise 3.1

For some of the particular virtues mentioned, e.g. courage and patience, describe how they can contribute to well-being if practised by:

1. The social care worker in seeking to accomplish his/her aims in a particular example of casework.
2. The client in relating to his/her care needs.

CASE STUDY 3.1

Case Study: Issue in Residential Care

You work in a residential centre for adults with learning challenges. The parents of Paul, who has a learning challenge, are unable to care for him at home any longer on account of their age. They wish to ensure Paul gets the care he needs as a permanent resident in the centre. However, they are concerned about the upset they will cause Paul if they tell him his stay in the centre is permanent and that he will not be coming home again except, perhaps, for an occasional visit. To avoid upsetting Paul, they have already explained to him that his stay in the centre is temporary and that he will be returning home when renovations to their home are complete, even though the house is not being renovated.

They ask you to go along with the explanation they have given Paul. They add that because of his learning challenges it is unlikely it will register with him over time that there must be another reason why he is not going home. They advise you that if he knows he will not be coming home then he is likely to become emotionally volatile. He may inflict harm on himself or strike out at staff or the other residents. They also fear he may withdraw into himself and never experience joy again.

Apply Aristotle's value of well-being to the response you would make to Paul's parents. Describe, in particular, the relevance that particular aspects of Aristotle's ethics have for the care of Paul if he is to achieve well-being.

CRITICAL EVALUATION

The Problem of Identifying Human Nature

Under Aristotle's ethics all human beings have the same function, i.e. to reason, and the same overall desire, i.e. to flourish as individual and social beings. We fulfil our function by making good decisions about managing our desires and feelings in order to flourish in accordance with the doctrine of the mean. This is the core of our human nature. Good conduct is in accordance with this understanding of our nature, while bad conduct goes against our nature as understood in this way. People's conduct can be judged to be good or bad, right or wrong, in the light of how well or badly they behave in relation to their human nature. If this view is true, it would provide a general, objective standard of ethical behaviour for all to follow.

However, it is a view that has been criticised. The main criticism disputes the idea that there is such a thing as human nature which can be identified with reason. Benn (1998: 163) points out that human beings are distinct from animal life in other ways besides being able to reason. For example, he cites a conscious desire to engage in sport or artistic pursuits as activities unique to human beings. Enjoyment of music could be considered a particular example because many people find it an essential part of their nature. Also, is reason unique to humans? In the light of the theory of evolution and study of animal behaviour in higher species, such as apes, it is not clear that having rational capacity is the distinctive feature of being human.

Benn points out that while reasoning is clearly important, and is arguably the main element characteristic of the human species, that does not mean we necessarily have to base our ethics on it in terms of using it to choose the virtuous response as a means to flourish. Fulfilling our plans and activities might just as easily enable us to flourish without regard for making rational choices to behave in accordance with virtue. In practice, many people identify their flourishing with the extent to which they realise their plans and activities.

The Existentialist View

In stark contrast to Aristotle, some modern philosophers hold that there is no such thing as a specifically human nature. This view is associated with some existentialist philosophers who came to prominence in France and Germany after the Second World War. They accept, of course, that human beings can and do use their reason. However, influenced by Nietzsche's ideas (1844–1900), they regard reason as under the sway of irrational desires, such as the desire for power.

The Holocaust of the Jews and other people by the Nazis during the Second World War is said to have influenced the existentialist view that we have no human nature. If people are supposed to be rational of their nature, how could some people deliberately set out to exterminate others? It makes no sense for people to exterminate their fellow human beings if they have a nature identified with rational behaviour which links them with everyone else.

Sartre (1905–80) takes the view that a person is to be understood precisely as lacking any nature. Instead of reason, Sartre speaks of our consciousness, but this consciousness is not anything. It is simply an emptiness or nothingness which we are compelled to try and fill by whatever takes our attention or by whatever desires we have. For Sartre, this is also what makes people free, as they are not bound by any particular nature (1995: 441). In the discussion in Chapter 7 about the value of empathy, we will go a bit more into the challenge people face in managing their freedom as one of the reasons for having understanding for them in the difficulties they experience.

A feature of life that came to prominence in the Western world, particularly during the twentieth century, and which is often described in modern literature, has been a sense of meaninglessness which people experience. Symptoms of a sense of the meaninglessness of individual and social life include behaving to excess as well as anxiety, depression and despair. In other words, people can feel alienated from themselves and their world. They do not feel at home in a psychological sense, but instead feel homeless. The absence of a human nature can be seen as lying behind this feeling since, if there was a human nature that was clear to people, it would give them a sense of having a personal core in relation to which they could find meaning and value in their lives.

The 'Open Question' Argument

Norman (1998: 33–4) makes a further criticism of Aristotle when he points out that even if we accept that reasoning is the defining function, or at least the *distinctive* or *characteristic* activity of being human, this does not necessarily imply that it is the kind of activity that is best for us. In other words, there is a philosophical problem of being able to prove that just because something *is the case*, i.e. that reasoning is our defining function, we therefore *ought* to behave in accordance with it. If we accept that everybody desires to flourish, we can still ask why they *ought* to do so. This is known as *the open question* argument. This is because when we say that something is the case, it remains an open question whether we should still behave in accordance with it. (See also 102; 160.)

But if we accept that we have a human nature, or at least a characteristic activity of reasoning which we identify with *being human*, it would still seem to be (in practice) a very good reason for behaving in accordance with it. We would at least be trying to act in conformity with ourselves rather than going against ourselves. At the same time, the distinction that is said to exist between something being the case and it having value raises a core problem in ethics. It is known as the *is/ought* or *fact/value* distinction. We will look at this problem again in Chapter 4.

REVIEW

For Aristotle, we achieve well-being through making rational decisions about our desires, taking account of our social nature as well. The rational decision is the midpoint of the desire between excess and deficiency. Decisions made in this way result in behaviour according to virtues such as courage. This view supports care practices such as empowering clients to make their own choices for well-being.

FURTHER READING

Banks, S. (2006) *Ethics and Values in Social Work*, 3rd ed., Palgrave Macmillan (Chapter 3).

Benn, P. (1998) *Ethics*, UCL Press (Chapter 7).
Goleman, D. (1996) *Emotional Intelligence: Why it Matters More than IQ*, Bloomsbury. (This is an interesting popular application of Aristotle's insight to everyday life.)
Norman, R. (1998) *The Moral Philosophers: An Introduction to Ethics*, 2nd ed., Oxford University Press (Chapter 3).

REFERENCES

Aristotle (1955) *The Ethics of Aristotle, The Nicomachean Ethics*, Penguin Classics. (**Note:** Classical ethical texts such as Aristotle's, referred to in this and other chapters, are available in more recent editions.)
Benn, P. (1998) *Ethics*, UCL Press.
Norman, R. (1998) *The Moral Philosophers: An Introduction to Ethics*, 2nd ed., Oxford University Press.
Nussbaum, Martha C. (1992) *Love's Knowledge: Essays on Philosophy and Literature*, Oxford University Press.
Sartre, J. (1995) *Being and Nothingness*, Routledge.

4
Respect and Care

OVERALL AIM

To show how the values of respecting others and caring for them can be considered basic moral principles that people are obliged to practise.

LEARNING OUTCOMES

At the end of this chapter you should be able to:

- Explain why Hume thinks we can't establish a convincing basis for morals for everyone because our judgments of right and wrong are based on feelings.
- Explain how, in contrast to Hume, Kant tries to show that there are moral principles everyone is obliged to follow, based on will and reason.
- Cite and explain two versions of Kant's categorical imperative which provide for universal moral principles based on will and reason.
- Arising from the categorical imperative, explain why respect for others is a basic principle and what it means for social care practice.
- Arising from the categorical imperative, explain why care for others is a basic principle and what it means for social care practice.

INTRODUCTION

However much people may recognise and accept that they should respect and care for others, it is often not borne out in practice, at the cost of much suffering. Reflecting on history, including recent history, will bring up many examples of people's inhumanity. The failure to respect the right of civilians to safety and security in conflict is a notable example. Also, in Ireland, concern has been expressed at incidences of racism following the increase in numbers of people of other nationalities now living and working in the country. There have also been cases of some employers paying immigrant workers less than the legal minimum wage. In medical care there is the example of some patients in Irish hospitals in 2005 and 2006, including terminally ill older people, having to be accommodated on trolleys in corridors due to overcrowding. In social care, an RTÉ *Prime Time* investigation in 2005 revealed seriously inadequate standards of care in a privately run nursing home for older people. The home was subsequently closed.

Respecting others means treating them as individual human beings. Care workers can come across situations where clients are not being treated with the respect to which they are entitled and this becomes an issue that needs to be addressed. Some examples of disrespect and bad care are obvious and the need for the practice to cease is clear. For example, it may be a case of an elderly person left to spend the night in a wheelchair because the staff cannot be bothered to help him/her to bed.

Other examples include lack of consultation with clients and not obtaining their agreement for matters that affect them, such as moving a resident in a home to another room or installing another bed for a second person in his/her room. Lack of respect can also include practices of doing basic personal tasks for clients out of convenience where they are capable of doing them for themselves given time, tasks such as tying the shoelaces of a person with a disability. Respect also includes respect for the emotional integrity of clients. This means they should not be treated in a patronising, condescending, ridiculing or embarrassing manner. Respect also means ensuring that rules in residential homes are not unnecessarily restrictive of residents' freedom.

If we can convincingly establish *why* we should respect others, this will provide a basis for helping to ensure that treating people with disrespect is not acceptable. The main philosopher who tried to establish why we should always respect others is Immanuel Kant (1724–1804). He claimed to prove that respect and care are moral principles everyone is obliged to follow. Before looking at his ideas, which can be difficult, it will be helpful to look at the problem he was trying to solve. This was the problem pointed out by David Hume, which is that we can't prove that there are obligatory values or principles for everyone.

DIFFICULTY IN ESTABLISHING A COMMON BASIS FOR ETHICS

From the evaluation of Aristotle's ethics, you may now have a sense of how radical philosophers can be in the questions they raise. Philosophers look for convincing arguments, for rational proof. If the conclusion is unpalatable, so be it. They take the view that it is better to be honest and accept the truth, as far as it can be known, than live under an illusion or wishful thinking.

Hume's View

A philosopher whose insight into the basis for our moral views convincingly shattered the wishful thinking of many people was David Hume (1711–76). Kant's ethics can be seen as an attempt to refute Hume's view. In trying to prove Hume's view wrong, Kant came up with one of the most important and influential ethical theories, a theory which has at its heart the principles of respecting other people along with caring for them. For this reason it will be helpful to look briefly at Hume's view.

Personal Feeling the Only Evidence

From a young age we are taught that actions such as theft and murder are wrong. This teaching is reinforced throughout our lives because it is the common and deeply held view that such actions are wrong. As a result, understanding that they are wrong comes to be inseparable in our minds from them as particular actions. Thus it can seem strange to have to consider that there may be little or no evidence to support the view that such actions are wrong. Hume is asking us to set aside what we have been taught and look for *evidence* that such actions are wrong. When we do so, he claims, we will see that there is no objective evidence. The only evidence why they are wrong is our *feeling* of disapproval for them. In thinking that the evidence for right and wrong resided in the nature of actions, unbeknown to ourselves, we were only referring to our own feelings about certain actions.

Hume invites us to examine any action to see where *right* or *wrong* lies. He says that no matter how hard we look, we will never find right or wrong in the action itself. Imagine you are walking down the street and see a man in front of you snatch a lady's purse and run off. You saw what he did (fact). You heard her shout, 'Stop, thief!' (fact). You see that she is hurt because she is crying (fact). But where do you see *wrong*? The *wrongness* of the action is not there as a fact in the same way as the other things you saw and heard are there as facts. So where is it? Hume argues that the wrongness of the action lies in your emotive reaction of disapproval for what the man did. Yes, your emotive reaction is a fact, but there is nothing about the action itself that makes it wrong as a fact or wrong as a result of any other evidence besides your emotive reaction. You may say, 'Hang on a minute, what about the law? Does that not make stealing wrong?' Yes, it does, but Hume would say we only have laws that make stealing wrong because in the first place we feel disapproval for it, particularly from fear of the harm it can cause us and others who have to live in society. In this way, for Hume, our moral judgments come from our feelings and not from our understanding of the actions themselves. He sums this up by saying 'morality is more properly felt than judged' (Hume 1969: 522). It's not that reason has no role. It can inform our understanding of an issue or condition that arouses our moral feeling, such as famine, and it can enable us to work out the best means to take action in accordance with our feeling. However, it is feeling which lies at the basis of our judgments.

Hume's view has been summed up for the way it points to a distinction between a fact and a value. It is known as *the fact/value distinction*. Facts and values are not the same thing. The only way they are connected is from the way our feelings about certain facts lead us to making value judgments about them.

Implications of Hume's View

If Hume is right, then he can be considered to have dealt a serious blow to the idea that there is a common morality that everyone has to follow, in particular that we should always respect others and care for them. This is because it follows from his understanding that morals can vary from person to person depending on how they happen to feel about particular actions. As he puts it, there is no way of showing that there are 'immutable measures of right and wrong that impose an obligation' (508). In effect, this means that there is no requirement for anyone to respect others and care for them unless they feel they want to. It's not that Hume is against values of respect and care, it's just that he believes we can't show why they have to be moral requirements for everyone.

If Hume is right, then this leaves a big problem for how we can ever expect people to behave according to certain standards. For example, if a person feels there is nothing wrong with allowing a person with a disability to go without a service he requires, we have to accept that his view is morally valid. This is because all that matters morally is how he happens to feel about it. We may, of course, disagree with him and give reasons for our disagreements, such as providing for equality, but at the end of the day, morally speaking, it is only our feeling against his.

KANT'S RESPONSE TO HUME

Agrees that Right and Wrong Do Not Come from the Nature of Actions

Kant felt challenged to respond to Hume's view. His challenge was how to prove that morality is not some free-for-all based on personal feeling. It was how to prove that we can still understand certain actions as right or wrong for everybody.

Initially, Kant agrees with Hume on one point. He says if we look for our principles in particular actions, it invariably results in those principles getting mixed up with our own self-interest. For example, the manager of a home for the elderly, while holding principles of respect and care, may see the practice of employing unqualified staff as acceptable because he can pay them less and therefore make more profit. Also, the manager of a residential centre for people with disabilities may see having minimal practices available to residents for their stimulation and development acceptable because it is administratively convenient. In such ways, Kant would see the danger in taking our cue for right and wrong from actions and practices. We may be inclined to look on those actions from the point of view of what suits us.

As a result, Kant says that the moral source must lie not in actions, but within ourselves as the agents of the actions. It is the only other available place to look. However, against Hume, Kant says that the source within ourselves does not lie in our feelings toward the actions. Our own feelings as a source would be even more likely to result in principles that serve our self-interest. Nor, for Kant, does the source lie within our inclinations and desires, for they, too, can be self-serving. It's not that our feelings or inclinations or desires, are necessarily bad, it's just they are not reliable guides and we need to eliminate them from having a role in determining the source of our values if we are to achieve certainty (Kant 1969: 55–6).

Where, then, does the source of our morals lie? Kant says the source of our morals lies in our *will*. To help with clarity, I have put the word *will* in italics when using it to refer to our human capacity of having a *will* or to the mental activity of *willing*.

Will

What is so special about our *will* that it can be the source of our morals? Kant's answer is that our *will* is the only thing that is always and absolutely good. 'It is impossible to conceive anything at all in the world, or even out of it, which can be taken as good without qualification, except a good *will*' (59). Hence it must lie at the foundation of morality. This is our *will*, considered first in itself as a human capacity. Kant considers it first independently of anything in particular that we *will* (60).

Two factors help to show that our *will* is the only thing good in itself. The first factor is that we do not have control over the consequences of our actions. So, when we *will* some action, even with the best *will* in the world, we can still cause bad consequences for others. For example, as a social care advocate, you may *will* that a client with a disability be set up in independent living because it will be good for him/her. However, in a particular case it may not turn out that independent living proves beneficial for the client – it could turn out badly.

To take another example, you may intend the best for an older person by helping him/her as much as possible, but you might be undermining the client's own ability to look after himself/herself and hence hastening the day when s/he will become even more dependant. It is for these reasons that Kant says our *will* as a capacity in itself, distinct from what we will, is the only absolute good.

You may say, 'But surely good qualities such as courage, self-discipline, dedication and loyalty, the qualities Aristotle regards as virtues, are good in themselves.' Not so. Kant points out that a person can develop such good qualities, but use them for a bad purpose (60). Benn gives the example of people who develop qualities such as loyalty, dedication and self-sacrifice to be more effective terrorists (1998: 102).

It is for these reasons, then, that good *will itself*, considered separately from anything in particular that it *wills*, is the first element that lies at the source of morality. The second element that lies at the source of morality is our human reason.

Reason

Kant accepts that there is a distinct human faculty of reason and that it has a role in controlling how we act. Nature has endowed us with reason as well as *will*, and reason is attached to *will* 'as its governor' (1969: 60). Reason's role is to be of service in producing, in practice, the one thing that is good in itself – the good *will*.

Will and Reason Together

So far, Kant's theory remains highly abstract. There are just two elements – good *will* itself and reason itself. It is what he calls purely *formal*. That is to say, it is empty of any specific content. But, so far, this is how he intends it to be. It is his method. Kant claims this abstract approach is necessary if we are ever to understand why there are moral principles that apply to everyone. In other words, he sees that we have to step right back from the particulars of our experience, or go to some place well above them, if we are ever to get an overall view of the source of moral behaviour for everyone. Of course, he does accept that in practice our *will* and reason aim at producing good actions. This is the whole purpose of morality. As we shall see, he claims to show us the supreme principle of morality (57). We can then apply it to decide what actions are right and wrong. Furthermore, he will give us examples of particular actions that are right or wrong in accordance with the supreme principle. But to get there, he first goes back to what he sees as the source of morality, which is independent of particular actions, and it lies in good *will* under the governance of reason.

The question then is, 'How does reason provide for a good *will* in practice?' Kant says it does so by enabling us to *will* actions that are *rational* as opposed to those based on feeling or inclination (62). A rational action that we *will* is one that won't involve us in a contradiction. This is Kant's key point: it would be contradictory to *will* the action as okay for ourselves but not for others. It is in this way that Kant arrives at the supreme moral principle. He calls it 'the categorical imperative'. In the next section we will take a closer look at it.

The Supreme Principle: The Categorical Imperative

'Categorical' means 'absolute' and 'imperative' means 'a demand'. Thus a categorical imperative is an absolute demand we have to follow in relation to how to behave morally. There is only one categorical imperative. It is so binding on us, Kant believes, that it has the force of law – not civil law, but moral law. He calls it 'a practical law' or 'the moral law' (83). It is not a law that society imposes on us for our own good, but a law we can recognise as valid from our own reasoning and therefore one that we should follow. Kant provides four different versions of the categorical imperative, each bringing out a different aspect of its meaning. We will focus on two versions. The first is the main one, and the second is concerned specifically with explaining why we are required to respect others. The main version is as follows:

> Act only on the maxim through which you can at the same time will that it should be a universal law.
>
> Kant: 84

A maxim is a particular principle upon which we act. It comes from our motive or intention to do something expressed as a principle. For example, if I intend to steal something, then I have to ask myself if I can rationally *will* my intention as a universal principle. That is, can I rationally *will* that it is okay for me, and for everyone, to steal? Or can I will that it is okay for me to tell a lie, and for everyone else? 'No,' says Kant, 'I can't *will* this because I would be acting in a contradictory way.' Kant explains the nature of the contradiction in detail. He says that if we did *will* a universal law that it is okay to tell a lie, then 'there could be no promises at all' since no one would trust that anyone is telling the truth. This means we could not lie successfully because no one would believe us. We would not succeed because people would naturally suspect we were lying to them since we have introduced a law permitting lying. We can only tell a lie and get away with it if there is an expectancy that others will believe we are telling the truth. This makes *willing* a law that it's okay to lie contradictory; it makes it *futile* or self-defeating. (In practice, as distinct from logic, we still might, of course, succeed in getting away with telling a lie by deceiving a person, but this is not Kant's point.)
Kant also explains the nature of the contradiction by pointing out that if we *will* a law to allow for telling lies, then we are *willing* a law from which we ourselves could become the victim. This is because if someone did happen to believe our lie,

once s/he found out that we had told him/her a lie, and that there was a law permitting lying, then s/he would be entitled to lie back to us. In Kant's phrase, s/he would be entitled to 'pay me back in like coin'. In other words, any law that I might *will* to tell lies would rebound on me. I would be putting myself into a position of being a victim. But who would want to *will* himself/herself to be a victim? To do so would be contradictory or irrational. Here is what Kant says:

> . . . I can indeed *will* to lie, but I can by no means *will* a universal law of lying; for by such a law there could properly be no promises at all, since it would be futile to profess a *will* for future action to others who would not believe my profession or who, if they do so over-hastily, would pay me back in like coin; and consequently my maxim, as soon as it was made a universal law, would be bound to annul itself.
>
> Kant: 68

Kant, then, is asking us to exercise our reason to see what we could *will*, not just for ourselves, but for everyone. We are being asked to think through what would happen, or what we would be signing up for, if we *will* that everyone could do the same as we are intending to do. In effect, the categorical imperative means that if you wish to do something, your action will be morally right if at the same time you can *will* that everybody else should do the same as you. On the other hand, your action will be morally wrong if you find you could not *will* that it should apply to everyone. It is always wrong to act in one way while wishing that no one else does the same.

Rationality, Not Consequences

Kant is sometimes misunderstood as arguing that the *consequences* of permitting everyone to tell lies would lead to social breakdown and that this is the reason why it is irrational. But Kant is not saying that to *will* to tell a lie is wrong because of its negative consequences on others or on society, and so we have to have a rule against lying in everyone's interest. This is the social convenience or social contract argument. But this is not Kant's argument. He would not consider this argument strong enough. No doubt he would acknowledge that negative social consequences are a good reason why we should not tell lies, but they do not *prove* why we should not. A person can still validly say, 'In my opinion I don't see anything wrong with telling a lie to suit myself when I want to, even if it has negative social consequences.' Kant wants to prove to such a person that his view is untenable. This is why he argues that in telling a lie a person is going against reason – reason that is common to every human being. Nor is he saying we would necessarily want to tell a lie and get away with it. He is merely pointing out the irrationality of wanting to do so.

'Do Unto Others . . . '

People sometimes remark on the similarity between Kant's imperative and the Christian principle of behaving toward others as you would like them to behave toward you. For example, we don't steal from others because we wouldn't want them to steal from us. There is a similarity, but Kant's imperative is based on a logical reason why we should behave in this way regardless of whether we accept the Christian moral teaching. He claims to provide a basis in a *law of reason* why we should treat others as we would like to be treated.

The Imperative as an Objective Criterion for Right and Wrong

With the categorical imperative, or supreme principle of morality, Kant is claiming that there is an objective criterion for deciding between right and wrong. Yes, a person can still ignore this criterion and behave in ways that go against it. However, in doing so he is behaving in a way that goes against his rational nature as a human being, which is common to everyone. Kant is pointing out to wrongdoers that they are in denial of what it is to be a rational human being. This, he claims, makes the reason why their behaviour is wrong *objectively* true, i.e. true for everyone no matter what their feelings or opinions are on the matter. In other words, what Kant is trying to show is that there are actions which are *wrong in themselves* and that people are going against *human* reason by doing them. This, Kant argues, give morals their *objective* force.

Respect and Care as Morally Required Principles

We have seen how the imperative applies to prove to us that certain actions are morally wrong and should be avoided. But how does the imperative or supreme principle apply to show us actions that are morally right, to the actions that we should do as distinct from actions we should refrain from doing? Kant picks two examples to look at, and they are that 'we should respect others' and that 'we should care for them'. Using the categorical imperative, he claims that he can prove the moral principle that we should both respect and care for others.

THE IMPERATIVE TO RESPECT OTHERS

The easiest way of understanding how Kant's imperative requires us to treat others with respect is to ask ourselves if we could *will* a universal law that everyone should be treated with respect. Our answer would have to be 'Yes'. Otherwise we would be willing a world in which it was okay for others to treat us with disrespect and this would make no sense.

However, there is a deeper reason why we have to respect others. If we take a closer look at the elements that make up Kant's supreme principle, we can see in those elements that everyone has an essential freedom and, as a result of this, deserves to be respected on the basis of equality. The following points show that everyone has a basic freedom and equality.

Will and Reason Common to All

Each person possesses a *will* and reasoning ability. Since we all have these capacities, they serve to identify a basic freedom and equality between everybody.

Everyone Decides

Morality is not imposed on us from without by some higher authority or institution. Each person is in the same position of addressing his/her own rationality to determine the actions which s/he can rationally *will* all others to do and those actions which s/he cannot rationally *will* others to do. Each is an authority in his/her own right to determine what is right and wrong in accordance with what can or cannot be rationally *willed*. There is an essential freedom and equality of everyone at the heart of the very process of determining moral principles. Kant calls this freedom the 'autonomy' of the individual.

Freedom to Obey or Disobey

Also, people are free in another sense. This is the sense in which they can choose to recognise, and try to live by, the moral principles that come from the categorical imperative or they can decide to not bother with them and suit themselves. Either way, their capacity to choose indicates their freedom. If they decide to ignore the principles that come from the imperative, they will then, as we saw, be acting against reason and in a morally wrong way (and perhaps breaking the state laws as well), but they will be indicating their human freedom. It's not that we should respect people for breaking the law! It's people's autonomy that deserves respect, for which breaking the law is an impermissible example. In particular, the autonomy at the heart of everyone points to the care requirement to treat with respect people who have broken the law and are detained in prison.

Moral Laws Apply to All Equally

As we have seen, the imperative requires us to consider right and wrong on the basis of being able to *will* the principles implied in our actions as *universal laws*. Since they have to be universal, this means they have to apply to everyone equally.

It would make no sense to will universal laws and make distinctions about who they should apply to on the basis of gender, skin colour, ethnic origin or disability.

Equality of Moral Status

Another way of saying that we all have an essential freedom and equality is to say that there is a basic or foundational equality of moral status among all people (90–91). To say that we have an equality of moral status is not to say that we are all equal in how moral we are. It is to say that considered as individuals, no one is better or inferior to anyone else by virtue of their status as a human being. This is an important point because not everyone, or every society, acts in a way that supports people having an equality of moral status. Discrimination, for example, is not treating people as having the same moral worth.

Treating People as 'Ends'

Kant describes the requirement to treat others with respect as a result of their autonomy by saying that we should always treat another person as an *end* in himself/herself. By *end* he means that we should see a person as free and autonomous in his own right. In practice we can say that to treat each person as an *end* is to treat them in a way that recognises their entitlement to make their own choices and decisions in pursuing their plans and activities. This essential freedom or autonomy is something we value in ourselves and it is necessarily how we have to understand the way others are for themselves. It requires that we avoid manipulating others for our own ends. In slavery, people are not treated as ends in themselves. Abusers fail to treat their victims as ends in themselves. This requirement to treat people as ends in themselves is particularly relevant in caring for those with disabilities, where there can be a tendency to restrict unnecessarily opportunities for them to live according to their own plans.

Of course, we also treat people as means to some end that we want. This is an inevitable part of human interaction. For example, we treat a taxi driver as a means to our end of taking us to our destination. In this sense, a care worker can be said to treat clients as a means to his/her end of accomplishing his/her work. However – and this is the crucial point – Kant says that we should never treat people 'simply as a means, but always *at the same time* as an end.' What Kant is saying, in effect, is that while using other people as a means, we should also have the greatest of respect for them as individuals. Here is the second version of the categorical imperative in full. It is called *The Formula of the End in Itself*. In ordinary language it is known as the *Respect for Persons* version of the imperative.

> Act in such a way that you always treat humanity, whether in your own person or in the person of any other, never simply as a means, but always at the same time as an end.
>
> Kant 1969: 91

This formula particularly brings out why it is morally wrong to ill-treat or abuse others. In doing so, a person is treating another as a thing or a tool for his own ends and not as an autonomous person who is an end in himself/herself as of right. This formula also highlights why all are deserving of equality of respect and treatment in society and in laws. It makes clear why many particular forms of behaviour that go against this basic equality are morally wrong. For example, people have rights under the law, so if their rights are being denied or withheld, this is to treat them with disrespect.

Kant's formula also requires that we treat *ourselves* as ends and have self-respect. For the same reasons as we have to respect others, we have to respect ourselves. It would make no sense to have to respect others while treating ourselves with disrespect. This duty includes developing our potential as best we can (92). This benefits not only ourselves but others also, since it puts us in a better position to be able to support and promote others in their needs.

THE IMPERATIVE TO CARE FOR OTHERS

Rationality, Not Self-interest

Kant claims there is a moral principle to care for others arising from the categorical imperative. He argues that we should *will* a universal law of care for others because we will require help some day. It is important not to misunderstand Kant when he says this. It is not that we should *will* care for others for a selfish or self-interested motive or, more generally, from a motive of common or collective self-interest. It is not a case of 'I'll help you provided you help me'. Nor is it even a case of 'one good turn deserves another'. The point is that, as for the example of lying, it would be self-defeating or contradictory or irrational to *will* into existence a law that no care should be given to others because then we would be *willing* that no care should be given to us when we need it. If we have *willed* that there is no obligation to help others, we are *willing* that no help should be given to us. Here is how Kant puts it: 'It is impossible to *will*' that we should do nothing for 'others who have to struggle with great hardships (and whom we could easily help).' This is the reason,

> For a *will* which decided in this way would be in conflict with itself, since many a situation might arise in which the man needed love and sympathy from

others, and in which, by such a law of nature sprung from his own *will*, he would rob himself of all hope of the help he wants for himself.

Kant 1969: 86

One way of expressing Kant's argument here is to say that the *effect* of the principle of acting to care for others is that others will (hopefully) care for us when we need it, but this is not the *reason* for the principle – the reason is that to disregard the principle is to act irrationally. We would be acting in a way that is inconsistent with our own *will*.

How Much Care?

Perfect Duties

Kant distinguishes between two types of obligations or duties under the imperative. The first type provides for a 'narrow (rigorous) duty'. This includes duties to refrain from lying or physically harming others. There is simply no two ways about having to observe them. They are called perfect duties from the fact that the requirement to abide by them is perfect or absolute. (Harming others in necessary self-defence could be considered an exception, as we have a duty to preserve and develop our own life.)

Imperfect Duties

The second type refers to 'wider (meritorious) duty' (86–7). This type of duty includes the duty to care for others. There are clearly many ways in which we can care for others, and we can do so to varying degrees. Kant calls caring 'an imperfect duty' because we can never fulfil it completely. Imperfect duties include a duty to develop our own potential. For Kant, this is also an imperfect duty because we can never fulfil it completely or in all ways. As O'Neill (1993: 178) puts it, 'We cannot help all others in all needed ways, nor can we develop all possible talents in ourselves. Hence these obligations are necessarily selective as well as indeterminate.' In other words, both how much care and in what way we give care are matters for us to decide and we have discretion in doing so. No one can specify for us either the nature of the care we are required to give or the amount.

Becoming Good by Providing Care

The fact that we have discretion does not mean we are required by the imperative to do only the minimum. Kant points out that the extent to which we discharge our imperfect duties is the extent to which we become good people. The more we seek to implement them to the best of our ability, the more we are doing the right thing and are behaving as well as we can, as a human being ought to behave. This is what makes us a good or virtuous person. We saw with Aristotle that there is no excess of virtue. For Kant also there is no excess of becoming virtuous through discharging our imperfect duties. In addition, we are only deserving of moral praise to the extent that we do more than the minimum (86–7). Schneewind makes the point that, if I want to, 'I may only do what is permissible within the limits of my legal duties', but 'I can become entitled to moral praise through my efforts for others. My merit increases as I make their goals my own' (1999: 324).

The Obligation to Provide Care

Example of Home Help Services

In a specific case of need, how are we to decide whether on not we have an obligation to provide care? For example, are we obliged to provide extensive home help services for an older person when s/he wants them, even though it would be more economical to care for him/her in a residential home where s/he is refusing to go?

Kant's answer would seem to be both 'No' (strictly speaking) and 'Yes'. 'No' because neither we nor the state can provide for the care needs of everyone in every respect. All we are obliged to do is provide some care, and this does not necessarily have to include providing elderly people with all the home help they may need. However, we (and the state on our behalf) are required to provide *some* care, and it is reasonable to conclude that this should include at the very least people's basic needs, of which you can argue independent living is one. In this way we can see how his answer could also be 'Yes'. In addition, by providing help, the state is acting in a way that is morally good and praiseworthy.

This line of argument can be applied to many other examples of basic care needs, including providing long-term accommodation for the homeless and helping them overcome the causes of their homelessness. Also, following Kant's line of thinking, it would be rational to *will* a universal law that those who need to be provided with independent living or a home should be provided with it, since we may need a similar provision for ourselves some day. Alternatively, since we can see we would want it for ourselves if we had the need, it is inconsistent of us to deny it for others.

DUTY ABOVE ALL

Duty is central to Kant's ethics. He argues that it follows from the existence of universal moral principles that we have a duty to obey them. It is probably true to say that many people today don't like the idea of duty. It is seen to run counter to the sense they have of their own freedom. Yet for Kant, morality is based on freedom. Each person, as we have seen, is a free or autonomous agent – but for Kant, freedom is not fulfilled through doing as we please. He understands freedom as the capacity to be motivated to act according to reason. Moreover, as Patton points out, Kant is saying that it is only when we act according to reason that we actually achieve real freedom (Patton 1969: 33). Then we are freed from being under the sway of inclinations and desires that are not reliable guides for moral behaviour. Freedom is fulfilled through doing our rationally recognised duties.

For this reason, for Kant, duty is more important than a natural, human inclination we may have to care for others. People now tend to be more at home with the idea that they behave well toward others, not because of duty, but because they feel for them and, in doing so, experience this as an uplifting expression of being human. But for Kant this is not a good enough reason. He goes so far as to say that good actions done *solely* out of inclination or feeling have 'no genuinely moral worth' (Kant 1969: 64). In order to have moral worth, they have to be done for the sake of duty. This is because duty comes directly from the source of morality in the *will* and reason, which gives us the categorical imperative. In addition, as we will see in the next section, for Kant it is dangerous to allow feeling or inclination to dictate what is right or wrong.

Remember, too, that people often lack the inclination to do the right thing. For this reason there is much moral weakness and moral failure in society. Kant's position on duty allows us to say that just because you don't feel like doing the right thing, this does not let you off the hook. Whether you like it or not, you have a duty to do the right thing.

This point goes to the nub of our experience of feeling morally challenged. When we experience moral challenge, we experience ourselves simultaneously pulled in the opposing ways of doing something we want to do and not doing it because we recognise it as wrong.

Why We Have to Set Aside Our Inclinations

One practical reason why we must put aside what is 'to the advantage of our inclinations' is because once we allow anyone to have such an advantage, then everyone will feel entitled to justify their actions by special motives they feel they have (87). Kant warns against this. He says we can all find ways of special pleading. The result would be morality ending up 'looking like anything you please' (89). So we must *will* a universal law impersonally 'without basing it on any impulsion or interest' (105).

For example, a branch bank manager who finds he is under intense pressure from headquarters to increase the branch's profits by overcharging may try to justify doing so by arguing that he is only following his superiors' orders or wishes, or by arguing that his career prospects will suffer if he doesn't. But this is only an example of special pleading. The same applies even in the hard case of a poor woman stealing food from a supermarket to provide for her children. She still has to put aside her (understandable) inclination, unless of course their very survival is at stake. She has to ask herself if she can *will* the principle arising from her intended action, which is that taking something that does not belong to her should be allowed as a moral law. Her answer has to be 'No'. Imagine if at the same time as she is taking the food from the shelf, her daughter, who had been at home, rushes up to tell her that a robber is in their house stealing their rent money. Logically, the woman would have to acknowledge that it is okay for the robber to take her rent. So, for Kant, we always have to put aside our inclination arising from our particular circumstances and base our judgment on the principle implied by the action we are intending.

Kant is pointing out that, if we want to, we can all try to find ways of arguing that our particular circumstances justify doing something we know is wrong. We see our circumstances as providing a justifiable exception to the rule. However, the reality is that we are only making excuses.

At the same time, we can argue, in the case of the poor woman (or other cases of a similar nature), that this logical answer does not adequately take account of the subjective reality of her plight given her particular circumstances. We can empathise with fact that she has felt driven to steal to provide for her children. Some critics say Kant's view is too rigid. It makes morality a matter of black and white with no shades of grey allowed. In practice, inclinations which arise from our circumstances often provide understandable human reasons why we behave as we do. After all, what if the woman finds her pride and dignity suffers unbearably if she has to seek charity or beg? It seems unreasonable of Kant not to accept circumstances in at least some hard cases as valid reasons which do not make an action wrong. We would say that, at the very least, circumstances can greatly reduce how wrong we consider the action to be, but a scale of wrongness is not something Kant includes. At the same time, his point is that to allow exceptions is to place ourselves on a slippery slope where we will have difficulty knowing how to stop allowing for exceptions.

Also, we should remember that where we have the means to relieve hardship, we have a duty to do so, admittedly an imperfect but meritorious one. So, under Kant's theory, other people (or society at large through the state's welfare system) can be considered lacking in morality through not having provided the woman with the help she obviously needs.

Kant's Positive View of the Role of Moral Feeling

It's important to emphasise that Kant is not against moral feeling and inclination having *any* role in morality. The main role he sees them having is as a feel-good factor which backs up or supports us when we have done the right thing, but it is not how we know we have acted in accordance with the moral law (120).

Secondly, Kant recognises that inclination has a role as a *motive* for doing the right thing as distinct from the reason for doing the right thing. He recognises that moral feelings clearly help people to do right and avoid wrong. As such, they are invaluable in practice. Patton makes this point:

> Furthermore he [Kant] never wavers in the belief that generous inclinations are a help in doing good actions, that for this reason it is a duty to cultivate them, and that without them a great moral adornment would be absent from the world.
>
> Patton 1969: 20

KANT'S ETHICS AND SOCIAL CARE

Respect for Others

Complete respect for others underlies the following four aspects of care work.

Self-determination

One immediate principle that follows from having complete respect is the client's right to make choices. Respecting a person means respecting their right to determine their own life as far as possible. This is an important guideline for care of people with disabilities and older people in particular. In relation to advocacy, self-determination includes empowering clients to become advocates for their own needs.

Equality of Treatment

This involves supporting the interests and rights claims of clients who have grounds for their case that they are not being treated equally or fairly under public policy. This may be for a number of general reasons, such as that there is no administrative provision under existing policy, that policy is not being interpreted correctly or that lack of resources is preventing the policy from being implemented. In other words, respect for persons underlies many practical issues that can arise around equality.

Informed Consent

In general, this means care workers should take account of the opinions and choices of clients. This includes ensuring, as far as possible, the client's informed consent for the care measures intended for him/her or for the nature and type of representation being proposed on behalf of his/her interests. Where the client may not be in a position to give this consent as a result of disability, for example, it should be obtained from his/her next of kin.

Qualified Confidentiality

Respect for clients also includes ensuring confidentiality. In practice, this means that information about a client and his/her circumstances should not be shared with anyone else, other than on a need-to-know basis. *Need-to-know* means where others will need to know the information in order to provide care for the client. This is particularly important in order to be able to act to investigate disclosures about abuse and, where abuse is occurring, to prevent it from continuing. In this way, confidentiality is never absolute, it is always qualified. It is important that clients know that while information they give will be treated in confidence, it will only be on this qualified basis. This is to ensure that there will be no mis-understanding. A problem can arise when confidentiality is assumed by the client to be absolute and s/he learns that information s/he shared has been passed on. This may be seen by him/her as a breach of trust and give rise to him/her withdrawing involvement and finding it difficult to trust again.

Related to confidentiality is respect for a client's right to privacy. Ensuring that clients have their needs of privacy met arises in particular in residential care.

Duty of Care

The idea of a duty of care informs and guides social care practice. A duty of care is central to the mission statement of care agencies and is much referred to by care practitioners. Most ethical theories provide reasons why we (or the state) should provide care. However, it is Kant's theory which provides a justification for a specific *duty of care*. Also, as we have seen, Kant explains why doing more than the minimum duty is morally good. O'Neill explains the implications of a duty to care by saying, 'A commitment of this nature, taken seriously, will demand much. If we honour it, we have on Kant's account shown respect for persons and specifically for human dignity' (1993: 179).

Duty of Self-respect

This is shown by, in particular, developing ourselves. Care workers seek to enable clients to develop themselves, and Kant can be seen as giving the reason why it is morally good to provide those in need with the opportunity for their self-development.

Responsibilities as Well as Rights

It is often said that we have responsibilities as well as rights. If we have a right to be respected, then we have a responsibility to respect other people. Kant's ethics helps us to understand why the fact that we have responsibilities as well as rights are two sides of the same coin.

Duty of Care and Advocacy

Kant's ethics on the duty to care helps us to understand the moral context of the work of social care advocates. This is because it is a matter of making the principle of caring for others apply to a particular need for care, for example, where an agency may not be willing (for lack of resources or other reasons) to grant a particular service. However, if a strong enough case is made, the agency may find a way of obtaining the required resources or of making a justifiable exception in the particular case. A society that has the resources to provide for at least basic care needs for those requiring them would seem morally obliged to do so as a universal law, and this provides justification for the advocate's efforts. By using the facts of the client's circumstances, the advocate tries to convince agency staff of the need for the service. In effect, the advocate is acting out of conviction that it should be a moral requirement.

Reporting Malpractice (Whistle-blowing)

Incidences of malpractice occur in all professions. This places an obligation on staff who become aware of any malpractice (or who have concerns that it might be occurring) to report it to the appropriate authority. It is desirable to have a charter that provides for it so that all staff are aware that it is a necessary and acceptable procedure and can be supported by the charter in making reports.

CASE STUDY 4.1

Case Studies: Freedom and Safety

Drawing on Kant's principles of respect and care, consider the appropriate response of the care team to the following situations. Include details relating to the client's level of challenge, and if certain conditions are proposed which support attendance, consider whether they adequately respect the client's freedom.

1. An eighteen-year-old with a learning challenge in a residential centre who insists on going into pubs in the town at night.

2. A seventeen-year-old with a learning challenge who wishes to attend a disco.

Consider and Discuss the Following Reported Cases in the Light of Kant's Principles of Respect and Care

1. THE MENTALLY ILL

The first comprehensive annual report by the Inspector of Mental Health Services for 2004 was critical of conditions in the Central Mental Hospital. Inspectors were critical of hygiene and said a lack of toilets meant that many patients had to slop out. The report also said there was a concentration on security rather than on therapy. In addition, it expressed concern that there were no clinical psychologists, occupational therapists, speech and language therapists or social workers within the services.

While the Director of the hospital said steps had been taken to improve conditions and that slopping out would soon cease, he also told RTÉ's *News at One* that it was 'a constant ethical struggle' to work in the environment and care for patients.

(Source: Carl O'Brien, Social Affairs Correspondent, *Irish Times*, 23 July 2005)

The standard of care in large psychiatric institutions was also severely criticised in the inspectors' report for 2005. Apart from the poor physical conditions in the institutions, it noted that in many wards patients have little or no therapeutic activity, multi-disciplinary input, regular physical or psychiatric assessment or care plans.

(Source: Carl O'Brien, Social Affairs Correspondent, *Irish Times*, 7 July 2006)

2. Needs of Disabled Boy Left Unmet

The Ombudsman for children dealt with a case in which a severely disabled fifteen-year-old boy was still confined to the downstairs living room of his home six years after applying for suitable accommodation. His mother was unable to carry him upstairs to the bathroom so all his needs had to be met in the living room. The Ombudsman reported that the boy had sent eleven letters to the relevant county council over four years but received only standard replies.

(Source: Marese McDonagh, *Irish Times*, 12 July 2006)

3. Disregard for Older People

In her report for 2004 the Ombudsman stated that many complaints she dealt with concerning older people stemmed from the failure of public bodies to pay due concern to the fact that complainants were elderly and might have difficulty in understanding complex forms or in obeying detailed regulations or guidelines about benefits or other schemes. She also criticised what she said was the general negative attitude toward ageing and the perception in richer Western countries that increased numbers of older people were a burden.

(Source: *Irish Times*, 6 July 2005)

Lack of attention to the needs of the elderly would seem to have played a part in the charges levied by The Department of Health and Children for almost thirty years prior to 2005 on those with medical cards who were in long-term residential care. The charges continued despite a Supreme Court finding in 1976 in the McInerney case that medical card holders could not be charged once there was an element of medical care involved.

CASE STUDY 4.2

Case Study: Treatment of Billy

Assume you are a new member of the care staff in a residential home for clients with particular physical and learning needs. Billy is a nineteen-year-old who appears generally unhappy and is easily upset. He complains about the food and says there is no choice and he frequently throws food or cutlery on the floor. When Billy becomes particularly upset, the practice has been for a staff member to insist that he go to his room and remain there until he has learned to behave himself.

Billy has noticeable speech and language difficulties, which make it difficult for him to communicate orally. In addition, he gets frustrated if asked to write points down and you have noticed that his literacy level is below that which would be expected of a nineteen-year-old. He has had speech and language therapy in the past, while attending school, but since he finished school last year the treatment stopped. Another staff member has said to you that Billy's problem is that he does not try and gives up too easily, with the result that he has lost some of the progress he had made. From talking to Billy, you are aware that he would like to do a computer course and have opportunities to meet and socialise with people his own age from outside the centre.

You brought up your concerns about Billy at the next staff meeting. However, none of the other staff felt there was anything further they should do for Billy. Some staff took the view that he was 'playing up' in order to get his way, and that provided they did not give in to his 'whims' he would learn in time to co-operate when he realised he could not get his own way. They added that the more attention they gave to him, the more he wanted. One staff member said she did not think Billy morally deserved any special consideration because he has been upsetting other clients.

You have also noticed that quieter clients are left to spend a large part of the day watching TV.

In giving your response to the case, explain the basis of the values and principles that inform and guide your response with particular reference to Kant's principles of respect and care.

Exercise 4.1

Identify an example from your own knowledge and experience of disrespect and/or lack of care shown to people who are in need of care in Ireland. Drawing on Kant's understanding of the moral requirements to respect and care for others, explain:

1. Why the lack of respect and care can be considered wrong.
2. What showing respect and care will mean in practice in the case.

CRITICAL EVALUATION

Abstract and Rigid: Overlooks Circumstances

A problem with Kant's principles is that he arrives at them through an exercise of pure reason without consideration of circumstances. In arriving at valid principles, we have to go only by our intention to do some act formulated as a universal principle, and not by particular circumstances. In the example of the woman who steals to feed her children, it is the principle that counts, not her circumstances. Kant doesn't allow for circumstances to influence how principles are to be understood in particular cases. However, in practice it is only within our understanding of particular circumstances that moral questions and issues arise for us. It is these circumstances which influence our application of the principles to particular cases. This is particularly so in social care decision-making. For example, the morally appropriate response of whether it is right or justified for the state to take into care the baby of a young mother with an addiction will depend greatly on the particular circumstances. Thus Kant's principles don't help us to understand the influence we should allow circumstances to have in guiding our application of the principles. At the same time, his principles do provide guiding benchmarks. It is only because we know we should have respect and care for both mother and child that the appropriate response is an issue in the particular circumstances.

Actually, we find that in complex circumstances different principles can contend with each other in their claim on us to give them the most weight, and we cannot decide to allow one principle to apply over another, or any combination of them, without being influenced by the circumstances. For example, in the case of a client with a disability who desires assistance to live independently, there are at least three principles that will lead to a morally appropriate decision either to provide the assistance with safeguards or not or to do so. On the side of a decision to provide the assistance are principles of respect for the client's autonomy to make his/her own choices and determine his/her own life, and the principle of providing care. However, on the side of turning down the client's request (or perhaps meeting it in a partial way which s/he considers inadequate) are principles of protecting the client from harm and perhaps also the principle of equality of treatment (if there is a question of providing preference to one client over others in the allocation of limited resources). Thus all these principles can be in the mix and contend with each other for our support, but the only way we can decide on which principle (or combination of principles) should guide the actual decision is by considering the particular circumstances of the case. In this case, circumstances could include the client's level of ability to cope in the judgment of the care team, the level of support, or opposition, from the client's parents and the availability of required services, etc.

Another way of explaining this difficulty with Kant's theory is to say that his theory is arrived at in the abstract, but morality only arises for us embedded in a set of circumstances. It therefore becomes a question of whether or not we can *will* principles as universal laws in their attachment to particular circumstances and not in the abstract. For more on this difficulty with Kant's theory, see Norman (1988: 79–81).

So, while Kant's principles can guide decision-making, his approach overlooks a crucial element: the details of the case. It's not that we could expect Kant (or anybody) to provide a detailed account of all the various types of circumstances that can arise which are relevant to moral decision-making in relation to his abstract principles, and then to tell us how much weight we are to give to them. It is that the factor itself of allowing moral weight to circumstances to guide the application of principles is not included in his theory. Other theories do allow for circumstances. In Aristotle's ethics, as we have seen, a good or virtuous decision depends on a person relating to his/her feelings and desires in the context of the particular circumstance that have aroused them, and in the context of the courses of action open to him/her.

The problem is also that, in practice, human situations can be complicated, so it is hard to have a rule that fits every case that will arise. We may find that circumstances require us to make justifiable exceptions to principles. Mill, whose Utilitarian Theory is examined in Chapter 6, makes this point:

> It is not the fault of any creed, but of the complicated nature of human affairs, that rules of conduct cannot be so framed as to require no exceptions, and that hardly any kind of action can safely be laid down as either always obligatory or always condemnable. There is no ethical creed which does not temper the rigidity of its laws, by giving a certain latitude, under the moral responsibility of the agent, for accommodation to peculiarities of circumstances.
>
> Mill 1944: 23

In other words, life can be more complex than principles allow for. However, in fairness to Kant's position, it needs to be emphasised that, as Patton points out, his main aim is to establish the principles according to which we should act. His aim is not the application of those principles to particular cases (1969: 15). It is therefore a matter of speculation regarding what he might or might not have thought about how his principles should be applied in the circumstances of specific cases. The few examples he gives are intended only as general illustrations. At the same time, as we have said, he does not make taking account of circumstances an integral part of deciding between right and wrong.

Provides Understanding for Common Moral Standards

Kant is said to have made one of the best attempts to demonstrate the commonly held view that the essence of morality lies in everyone having the same standards. This is something that accords with people's general understanding and expectancy. As Patton points out, this is at the heart of Kant's ethics: 'He [Kant] holds that a man is morally good, not so far as he acts from passion or self-interest, but so far as he acts from an impersonal principle valid for others as well as himself. This is the essence of morality' (1969: 30).

Provides Rational Understanding of Guilt

Some people may feel Kant's moral laws are unduly restrictive, and that the primary good is to fulfil ourselves in achieving our plans even if it requires us to do things we could not agree that others should be allowed to do. However, Kant's point is that if we do so, we are not really fulfilling ourselves because we are going against our rational nature as human beings. So, if we are feeling guilty, it is understandable because we are recognising that we are behaving in a way that no one should. One of the merits of Kant's theory is that it provides a rational explanation for the psychological experience of moral guilt.

Distinction between an Action being Contradictory and Wrong

This criticism requires making a fine distinction, which may be hard to see. The distinction was pointed out first by another famous philosopher, Hegel (Norman 1998: 81–2). If our behaviour is contradictory, does this also make it wrong? Hegel pointed out that it is not the same thing to say an action is contradictory and to say it is wrong. To see the distinction, we need to look a bit more closely at Kant's argument. Kant argues we could not rationally *will* a universal law that permitted telling lies because then no one would trust that anyone else was telling the truth, so it would be logically impossible to succeed in telling a lie as others would be wise to the fact. If you like, such a law would collapse from being contradictory. Also, we would, in effect, be *willing* as acceptable a practice by which we ourselves could become a victim of someone lying to us, which would be an irrational thing to do. In this way, Kant's argument claims to prove that telling lies is wrong. But does this argument prove it wrong? Yes, it would be contradictory for anyone to *will* a law that it is okay to tell lies, but this does not necessarily make it wrong. You can argue that Kant assumes that *because* lying is contradictory that this *makes* it wrong, but an action being wrong can be regarded as different to it being contradictory. When Kant points out that it is contradictory to tell a lie, he is taking for granted that lying is wrong, that there is something bad about it, but he is not proving it to be wrong. While Kant certainly offers a good reason why we should not lie, it is not a reason that shows lying to be wrong as such. This criticism can also be applied to show that Kant does not prove to us why respect and care are moral principles we have to follow, even though he gives us good reasons for doing so.

Assumes Free Will

Kant's theory depends on accepting that our *will* is free in being able to *will* rationally principles as universal laws without being influenced by anything else.

The *will* has to be pure, detached from any motive or desires we may have. Otherwise, their influence will enter into *willing* universal laws, making them personal and subjective to us rather than objective for all. But he has great difficulty showing that we have free will. This is a point we will look at more closely in Chapter 7, where people's lack of free will is considered as one reason why having empathy for them is understandable as a value.

REVIEW

Kant tries to show how moral responses have a solid foundation. This foundation lies in the principle of regarding those actions as morally right which we can rationally *will* as universal laws and those actions as morally wrong which we cannot *will* as universal laws. From this principle comes the obligation or duty to comply with moral laws. These duties include a duty to respect others and to care for them.

FURTHER READING

Banks, S. (2006) *Ethics and Values in Social Work*, 3rd ed., Palgrave Macmillan (Chapter 2).
Benn, P. (1998) *Ethics*, UCL Press (Chapter 4).
Glover, J. (1999) *Humanity: A Moral History of the Twentieth Century*, Jonathan Cape. ('A Study of Ethics and Inhumanity'.)
Norman, R. (1998) *The Moral Philosophers: An Introduction to Ethics*, 2nd ed., Oxford University Press (Chapter 6 on 'Kant' and Chapter 10 on 'Facts and Values').

REFERENCES

Hume, D. (1969) *A Treatise of Human Nature*, Penguin Classics.
Kant, I. (1969) *The Moral Law: Kant's Groundwork of the Metaphysic of Morals*, translated and analysed by H. Patton, Hutcheson University Library, London.
O'Neill, O. (2004) 'Kantian Ethics' in *A Companion to Ethics*, P. Singer (ed.), Blackwell.
Patton, H. (1969) 'Analysis of the Argument' in *The Moral Law: Kant's Groundwork of the Metaphysic of Morals*, Hutcheson University Library, London.
Schneewind, J. (1999) 'Autonomy, Obligation and Virtue' in *The Cambridge Companion to Kant*, Cambridge University Press.

5
Human Rights

OVERALL AIM

To explore the basis for human rights as well as their moral and legal force in practice for social care.

LEARNING OUTCOMES

At the end of this chapter you should be able to:

- Appreciate rights as a force for social and political change.
- Explain how the existence of rights has been justified by natural law theory and by Kant's duty theory.
- Show familiarity with the main rights relating to care in international agreements and Irish law.
- Understand and assess the value of rights for particular care provision, such as equality of treatment for people with disabilities and provision of basic living standards.
- Explain the theoretical difficulty in proving rights exist.

INTRODUCTION

Of all ethical ideas, the idea that everybody has certain rights has come to have the most practical significance. This is because there is a general acceptance that where a right can be shown to exist, it must be met, as far as possible. In particular, governments are seen as having an obligation to provide for and uphold the rights of all citizens. Mill makes this point well:

> When we call anything a person's right, we mean that he has a valid claim on society to protect him in the possession of it, either by the force of law, or by that of education and opinion. If he has what we consider a sufficient claim, on whatever account, to have something guaranteed to him by society, we say he

has a right to it. If we desire to prove that anything does not belong to him by right, we think this done as soon as it is admitted that society ought not to take measures for securing it to him, but should leave him to chance, or to his own exertions.

Mill 1944: 49–50

Almond points out the practical relevance of rights:

Appeal to rights is widely understood and accepted everywhere in the world under all types of political regime. It is no small advantage to a moral notion that it should be regarded as valid across so many nations and cultures, and that it should have at least the potential of binding governments to the observation of important moral constraints.

Almond 2004: 263–4

Where a right is established, it usually receives the backing of law. This cements its practical significance in place. Under international law, for example, there is a right to asylum for a person whose circumstances meet the requirements. In Ireland, equality rights are provided under the Employment Equality Acts of 1998 and 2004. These Acts prohibit discrimination in the workplace. The Equal Status Acts of 2000 and 2004 prohibit discrimination in the provision of goods and services, accommodation and education. This legal provision in domestic law of some rights gives them a particular practical significance.

The care worker can come across issues relating to rights in providing care. It may, for example, be a case of a family from an ethnic minority or Travelling community experiencing discrimination in trying to get accommodation or places for their children in a crèche or school, and where reasons other than discriminatory ones are used as a pretext. Also, as we shall see, under the EU charter people have a right to the protection of social welfare where they cannot provide for themselves, and care workers can come across cases where clients may not be receiving the welfare support they are entitled to have. Also, in providing family support services in cases where parents have separated, care workers need to ensure the rights of both fathers and mothers to be involved in continued care for their children and in care plans for them.

HISTORICAL SOURCE

How is the idea that we all have rights justified? One way ethics tries to justify rights is on the basis that there exists what are called *natural laws* which should govern relations between people. These laws come from basic human inclinations common to everyone. Recognition of natural law goes back over 2,000 years when it emerged in ancient Greece. It was prominent in both Greek, and later Roman,

Stoic philosophy where there was a notion of universal brotherhood based on the recognition that people have a common human nature identified with having rationality along with basic natural inclinations or desires.

Natural is contrasted with the notion of *convention*. In other words, natural law is not something regarded as made up for human convenience, like the idea of the social contract, which we will be looking at in Chapter 10. Instead, natural law is something we are said to be able to recognise as existing of itself and providing an absolute standard for understanding actions that are right or wrong. In the same way that there are obvious features naturally occurring in nature, such as day and night, the seasons and the movement of the planets, natural law theory claims that there are obvious features to human behaviour that are natural and from which we can derive natural laws. So, by *natural rights* is meant the existence of rights or entitlements that arise from the basic natural inclinations of human beings. People are said to have these rights simply by virtue of being born as a human person. They are regarded as both fundamental and having universal validity.

Arising from the idea of a common human nature is the idea of human equality, that is, the idea that there is an *equality* of *moral status* shared by everyone regardless of differences in their capacity or position in society. 'Human equality is the direct consequence of natural law, its first and essential tenet' (d'Entreves 1964: 22). Also directly linked to natural law is the idea of the *intrinsic value* of each person, regardless of their abilities or social status (54).

The idea that everyone has natural rights, especially in relation to an equality of moral status, has been a powerful force in history. It has provided justification for people to strive to give practical expression to the idea of equality by taking action against conditions of inequality where they existed socially and politically. In other words, people have sought to change conditions under which they felt some people were not valued equally. Natural law has provided this justification because it has been seen as more basic than state law and having the authority to direct state law. The idea of natural rights lay behind both the American Revolution of 1776 and the French Revolution of 1789, both of which highlighted the natural law basis of human rights in their declarations (60). For d'Entreves, the revolutions turned the idea of natural law into a theory of natural or human rights, and for practical purposes natural law theory since then has been a theory of rights (59).

In addition, in its origin, and for much of its history, natural law was linked to belief in God as the creator of nature. Natural law was seen as an expression of divine providence. This belief is not essential to acceptance of the theory, but it did, and does for those who subscribe to it, give to natural law a further reason for regarding it as the ultimate authority for both morals and state law. One philosopher who spelled out the provisions of natural law was Thomas Aquinas. We will look briefly at his theory next.

Aquinas's Natural Law Theory

For Aquinas (1225–74), natural law, properly speaking, can only be understood as arising from reason. It takes reason to recognise that something is natural. The provisions of natural law come from reason reflecting on natural human inclinations, and there are three basic inclinations arising from one overall inclination, which is our inclination to do good and avoid evil.

The first natural inclination a person has is to preserve his own existence (self-preservation). It is, if you like, the most basic human instinct. Through our reason reflecting on this inclination, Aquinas claims it can be seen that those actions are naturally good by which a person's life is preserved and his death avoided. From this comes the first provision of natural law, which is that life should be preserved. The second natural inclination we have is to mate and bring up children. Through reason reflecting on this inclination, it can be seen that those actions are good which relate to men and women having and bringing up children. The third natural inclination we have is to live in society. Through reason reflecting on this inclination, we can see that those actions are good which sustain a society (Baumgarth and Regan 1998: 46–8, and for an account Copleston 1957: 214–5). So, if these are three precepts of natural law, how do they relate to natural or human rights? For Aquinas, because all people have the same basic inclinations, there are natural rights relating to what is just on the basis of equality (1988: 138–40). In particular, you can argue that from the first natural law to preserve life comes certain fundamental rights, for example, the right to life and also a right to the practical means to preserve life, means such as adequate food and shelter since they are necessary to provide basic security and protection, without which life would be at risk. Also, from the second natural law relating to procreation, you can argue it is rational to conclude that children, for example, have a right to protection and to basic education and of families to basic social services where they cannot provide for themselves, such as an income in unemployment and in old age. From the natural law relating to living in society, you can derive the right not to suffer discrimination. In this way, rights are seen as based in natural law theory.

Aquinas's Theory and the Modern View of Rights

I have emphasised how natural law provisions in Aquinas's system can give rise to certain economic and social rights which are recognised today. However, Aquinas's system is a system of natural law, not a system that emphasises rights (d'Entreves 1964: 45–6). Aquinas's theory is based on his view of the proper way to live in accordance with the natural law which, as a Catholic theologian, philosopher and saint, he regarded as participating in divine law. Aquinas's theory was not for the purpose of providing the modern, secular view of the rights, the view that fuelled revolutions and that is now the main moral appeal for social improvements. The reason I have focused on his theory is for the way it enables us to see how human rights might be justified in nature. Also, it shares common ground with the modern view of rights. This can be seen today in particular in the emphasis church representatives place on the dignity and worth of each individual and in their criticism of social conditions that undermine that dignity and worth.

Natural Law and Catholic Morality

Aquinas's natural law theory is also notable because it is one of the contributory sources to some of the moral views of the Catholic Church. The Church's views have had, and continue to have, a significant influence, especially on the moral values of many in Irish society. For example, Aquinas's understanding of the natural law basis of morality is one of the sources behind the Church's view that human life begins at conception and the unborn has a right to protection from that stage, with the result that abortion is morally wrong. It is also one source behind the Church's view that artificial contraception and gay and lesbian sexuality are morally wrong. As a contributory source to such moral views, the theory is open to question. Buckle, for example, argues that natural law's basic precepts are too general to be able to link specific practices to them in a way that proves the practices are wrong. For example, he would see it as unjustified to argue that because people naturally desire to procreate that artificial contraception is wrong for this reason. Sexual intercourse can have natural purposes other than procreation. Also, he argues generally that this natural law theory takes a narrow biological view of human nature, overlooking natural desires humans have such as for sexual pleasure, love, security and fulfilment (2004: 'Natural Law' 170–73). Parekh, too, would see the way Aquinas understands human nature as limited in the kinds of things it regards as natural. Parekh does not subscribe to natural law, but he does provide a richer account of human nature and sees it having a normative function, i.e. a function of indicating to us what our values should be. His account includes a range of natural human mental and emotional capacities, such as self-reflection, falling in and out of love, desiring to be respected and the awareness of growing old and dying (2000: 114–26). He also takes account of the idea that the kinds of things we consider natural are in part shaped by our culture as well as our nature. We will look at his view again in Chapter 8 on the value of accepting moral difference.

The views of both those who take their morality from natural law, as Aquinas understands it, and those who don't contribute to the moral climate of Irish society. A point to note is that the state, through the courts, recognises that there are different viewpoints and that it has no justification for giving priority to moral requirements arising from a particular understanding of natural law. This arose in 1995 in the constitutional challenge to the Irish government's abortion information legislation. Counsel representing the pro-life view argued in the

Supreme Court that the abortion information bill was unlawful because under natural law the unborn's right to life was superior to any man-made law or constitution. Any law which violated this right to life must be wrong, even if the people voted for it in a referendum. The Court rejected this argument. It recognised that in a pluralist society people differ in their moral views and that the Court cannot be guided by one view of natural law. Instead the Court has to go by the provisions of the Constitution, which are the basic laws for which the people have voted.

Rights as Moral Qualities

We have seen that, for practical purposes, it was the French and American revolutions which turned the idea of natural law into a theory of human rights. But it was Hugo Grotius (1583–1645), a leading natural law philosopher, who is said to have first interpreted natural law provisions specifically as rights provisions. From him comes the idea that 'a right is a moral quality of a person'. He believed a right is a quality we have similar to the way we have physical qualities such as a brain or a heart. For Grotius, the big significance of having rights is that they confer the authority of law on what we can do or on what we can have. A right provides legal entitlement even where the law of the state does not, or has not yet, supported it in legislation (Buckle 2004: 168).

Support for Rights from Kant's Ethics

Kant's moral theory is also seen as a source for human rights, particularly for equality rights. This arises from his understanding, as we saw, of people being equal in their moral status from having an essential freedom or autonomy. If we accept Kant's argument that there is an equality of moral status among everyone, then we can argue that equality rights exist.

MAIN SOCIAL CARE PROVISIONS IN HUMAN RIGHTS AGREEMENTS

There is a long list of things for which it is recognised that people have rights. What follows are some rights of relevance to social care provision in Ireland.

The United Nations Declaration of Human Rights

This dates from 1948. In 1976, it was amended and divided into a list of *Civil and Political Rights* and *Economic, Social and Cultural Rights*. It is the economic, social and cultural rights that are of particular relevance to social care.

A key phrase in Article 23 (3) of the Declaration states that people have a right to 'an existence worthy of human dignity'. This is a general phrase and open to interpretation, but suffering and death from preventable disease and food shortage, which is the plight of many in the world, is clearly not an existence worthy of human dignity and so people in such circumstances have a right to assistance.

Specifically, Article 11.2 of the Covenant on Economic, Social and Cultural Rights recognises 'the fundamental right of everyone to be free of hunger.' Article 11.1 'recognises the right of everyone to an adequate standard of living for himself and his family, including adequate food, clothing and housing, and the continued improvement in living conditions.' Other articles recognise rights to health, physical and mental (12.1), and education (13). These provisions recognise a right everyone has to a level of income and social care services needed to have an adequate standard of living where they cannot provide for themselves.

The European Convention on Human Rights (ECHR)

This dates from 1950 and is a particularly influential agreement. It predates the European Union and is not an EU agreement, but all member states are included among those who signed up to it. The Maastricht Treaty includes an article stating that the EU shall respect fundamental rights as granted by the Convention. Also, the EU Court of Justice takes the Convention as the source for upholding rights within the EU. In addition, EU states have agreed that members shall comply with the Convention (Dinan 2005: 290–91).

Ireland introduced legislation to give legal effect to the European Convention in Irish law. This was done in the European Convention on Human Rights Act 2003.

Article 3 of the European Convention states no one shall be subjected to 'inhuman or degrading treatment'. We will look at what this might mean in practice in the section on the effectiveness of agreements.

Charter of Fundamental Rights of the European Union

This is the EU's own human rights agreement. It was adopted by all member states in 2000. It is quite explicit in recognising social services as a right, and the intention was to give it legal status by incorporating it into the proposed EU Constitution. However, the Constitution is at present on hold following its rejection in referenda by the people of Holland and France. Nevertheless, the Charter is already in use. It is cited by both applicants before the EU Court of Justice and by the Court itself in its decisions. Dinan points out that the impact of the Charter on EU law 'remains to be seen, but is likely to be formidable' (2005: 291–2).

Article 34 of the Charter provides a right to social security and social assistance to ensure protection and to prevent social exclusion. The right to social and housing assistance is specifically mentioned in subsection 3.

Children's Rights

Of particular note is Article 24 of the Charter, which deals with the rights of children. It states that:

'(1)   Children shall have the right to such protection and care as is necessary for their well-being. They may express their views freely. Such views shall be taken into consideration on matters which concern them in accordance with their age and maturity.

(2)   In all actions relating to children, whether taken by public authorities or private institutions, the child's best interests must be a primary consideration.'

Children's rights are also provided for under the UN Convention on the Rights of the Child. This is a particularly important document for the worldwide protection of children. It sets out children's rights. One example is Article 37 (C). It provides for the right of children (those under eighteen) who are detained by the state under the law to be held separately from adults, unless it is in their best interests.

Children in Irish Jails

'We have 250 young people a year going into adult prisons, which does not sound like a big deal, but if you are fifteen an adult prison is quite a scary place to be.' Emily Logan, Ombudsman for Children.

(Source: Marese McDonagh, *Irish Times*, 12 July 2006)

In 2007 the government published for debate proposed changes to the Constitution with a view to holding a referendum to improve children's rights, notably in relation to their parents' rights. Proposals include the direct affirmation of 'the natural and imprescriptible rights of all children'. Proposals are intended to enable the State to be better able to meet a child's best interest in exceptional cases where parents have failed in their duty towards their child. Cases would include court decisions relating to the custody of, and access to, a child of separated couples. Measures are also proposed to give children greater protection against offences.

Rights of Older People

Article 25 of the EU Charter states, 'The Union recognises and respects the rights of the elderly to lead a life of dignity and independence and to participate in social and cultural life.'

Rights of People with Disabilities

Article 26 of the EU Charter states, 'The Union recognises and respects the right of persons with disabilities to benefit from measures designed to ensure their independence, social and occupational integration and participation in the life of the community.'

The draft of a UN treaty on the rights of people with disabilities was agreed in 2006 and is expected to be ratified in due course. Its provisions include a requirement on all countries to have laws banning discrimination against people with disabilities and a requirement to make essential equipment affordable.

Human Rights Commission Act 2000

This Act set up a commission to oversee the protection of human rights in Ireland. Among the purposes of the commission are:

8 (a) 'To keep under review the adequacy of the law and practice in the State relating to the protection of human rights.'

It also has as its purpose to conduct enquiries and to promote understanding of the importance of human rights.

EFFECTIVENESS OF AGREEMENTS

In view of human rights agreements, you may be wondering why it is that the rights of some people are not provided for in practice. For example, why are there still people homeless if the UN covenant says people have a right to adequate housing? Also, having to sleep rough is not an 'existence worthy of human dignity', and people have a right to such an 'existence' under the UN Declaration. You would think, too, that having to sleep rough is 'inhuman and degrading treatment' and so goes against a person's rights under the European Convention. Also, why are people with disabilities left without access to services to integrate them with the community if, as the EU Charter states, they have a right to benefit from such services?

The central question here is this: 'If a client has a human right to something, does this mean the state has to provide him with it?' The answer is 'Yes' if the right in question has been turned into a legal right by the laws of the state. Basic civil and political rights are also legal rights in the Irish justice system. For example, a right to vote, to freedom of speech and to equality before the law is provided for under the Constitution, which lays down the state's basic laws. Also, there are a number of specific laws prohibiting discrimination, so under the provisions of such laws a person has a legal entitlement, enforceable through the courts, to these rights.

However, the answer is not a straightforward 'Yes' in relation to what are called 'economic and social rights'. The reason for this is because international law 'still allows states considerable latitude to adopt administrative remedies provided those remedies are *timely, accessible, affordable and effective*.' This was the observation of the Human Rights Commission in May 2003 on the Irish Disability Bill (Quinn 2004). In effect, this means that governments have leeway in providing people with their social and economic rights provided by international agreements. Under Article 2 of the covenant, legal obligation on governments is 'to take steps . . . with a view to achieving the full realization' of rights.

From a service user's perspective, the problem with this is that it allows governments off the hook with regard to making sure the required services are provided as a matter of priority. From the government's perspective, however, 'progressive achievement' recognises the reality of the cost implications of providing the services, particularly in the light of other demands on government spending.

At the same time, governments could, of course, further their obligation under international law to progressively achieve implementation of economic and social rights by introducing laws that specifically provide people with services as of right just as they have laws that provide a right not to suffer discrimination. This would then mean a service user would have an automatic legal (as well as moral) entitlement to that service. It would mean that if a government was not providing the service, then the service user would have clear legal grounds on which to force the government through the courts to provide the service.

This is why the government's European Convention on Human Rights Act 2003 is seen as particularly significant, as it gives effect in Irish law to the provisions of the European Convention. Rights under this Act, which include, as mentioned, the right not to suffer inhuman or degrading treatment, have direct legal force. So it could be argued, for example, that to leave people with autism without a required service which would help lessen the difficulties they have in coping with their life is inhuman and degrading treatment. Can you think of other examples of conditions that people experience in Ireland that could be interpreted as treating them in a way that is inhuman and degrading?

Another point to note is the meaning of the precise wording in legal provisions. For example, in the EU Charter people have a right to housing *assistance*, which is not the same as having a right to be provided with a house. Also in the EU Charter, people with disabilities have a right *to benefit from measures* designed to ensure their independence and integration, which is not the same as having a right to those measures in the sense that a government has to provide them. However, the spirit of the agreements, as distinct from the letter, is to do as much as possible to ensure that people's economic and social rights are met in practice, and this *spirit* can be important in how a court interprets a provision in a particular case.

RIGHTS IN RELATION TO SERVICES FOR PEOPLE WITH DISABILITIES

The Rights View

A key question for advocates representing people with disabilities is whether disabled people have a right to the services they need in order to have the same (or as close as possible) level of equality of opportunity that able-bodied people enjoy. Groups representing people with disabilities sought to have legal provision of services incorporated in the government's Disability Act 2005 as of right. They argued that, as things stand, the disabled don't have the same rights as everyone else. This is because society does not provide services for their particular needs in a way comparable to the services provided for the needs of the rest of citizens.

The main point in this argument is the right of disabled people to equal treatment, which for them means having their particular needs provided for so that they can be in the same position as everybody else as far as possible. We live in a society that is organised primarily for the benefit of people who don't have a disability. Health and education services and access to transport and buildings are provided for the majority. However, people with a disability live in a society that is not organised in a comparable way for their benefit. For example, if they have particular education, health or development needs, society is not organised to meet their needs in a similar way to the way it is organised to meet the needs of the rest of citizens in these areas. You can argue that a child with speaking difficulties has an automatic right to the services of a speech and language therapist in order to benefit from their right to a primary education in a way comparable to children without language difficulties. You can argue that a deaf child has an automatic right to have all classes in school provided in sign language and a blind child to have all reading material provided in Braille. As has often been pointed out, if the majority had speech and language difficulties or autism, there would be little question that state services to help overcome these difficulties would be in place, and that people would be seen as having a moral and legal right to such services. So, through lack of access to special needs services, you can argue that the minority with special needs are not being placed on an equal footing with everyone else as far as is possible. There are, of course, special needs services, and there are measures in place to provide for the access to transport and buildings. There is recognition that people with special needs are entitled to such services and there is legal provision for services. However, entitlement to have these *provided in practice* automatically is not seen as a legal right. Much remains to be done to ensure that people do, in fact, get the services they need.

The extent to which the disabled lack the provision of such services is the extent to which they are said to suffer unequal treatment in society. They are equal members of society who, through no fault of their own, need special services to be able to benefit from society as closely as possible to the way everyone else benefits. If denied those services, they are at an unfair disadvantage. So, for the basic reason of equality, people with disabilities argue they have legal rights not merely to particular services, but to have those services provided *in practice* as of right.

Government's Response to Rights Request for Disability Services

The government argued that it could not provide services as of right because it would be too costly. Instead, under the Disability Act, there is a legal entitlement to an independent needs assessment for each individual, as well as entitlement to complaints and appeals procedures. A person with a disability also has legal entitlement to be represented by a personal advocate to work on their behalf for the provision of services. However, there is no automatic legal entitlement to have the actual services themselves provided, services which have been determined to meet the assessment of needs. For health and education needs, provision is subject to regard for 'the practicality' of providing the services as well as regard for meeting the cost within the year's overall financial allocation for services. In effect, instead of getting services for identified needs as of right, people with disabilities will get them subject to resources and where practicable. The same limiting factors of cost and practicability also apply for the legal entitlement of people with disabilities to have services provided for them by public bodies in ways that meet their special needs, services such as making information available in media which they can access.

WHO IS RIGHT ABOUT DISABILITY RIGHTS?

One argument made against people with disabilities, and people with welfare needs in general, having an automatic right to be provided with services is that it clashes with the right that others claim they have to be entitled to their wealth and not have it taxed in order to pay for those services. In Chapter 11 on social justice we will see that Nozick makes this argument in relation to welfare services generally.

In practice, however, the main point in the argument against people with disabilities having a right draws from the notion of what Mill calls 'public expediency', and this, in effect, was the government's argument. This is the argument that if providing services for everyone's disability needs is not feasible given the practical implications of doing so, then a right to those services may not have to be provided. It is the argument that providing for them is limited by 'the inevitable conditions of human life, and the general interest' (1944: 58–9).

This is the argument that the government made in saying that society as a whole could not bear the cost of providing such services. To provide the services would be to burden the taxpayer too much or lead to an unacceptable reduction in public provision of other services. However, whether this would or would not be the result in the case of disability services is debatable.

Also, an important factor which Mill points out is that the argument from public expediency is not set in stone. It is an argument that has always been made against granting to people what they claimed were their rights, and, for a time, public expediency stood in the way of something becoming a right that eventually did become a right.

> The entire history of social improvement has been a series of transitions, by which one custom or institution after another, from being a supposed primary necessity for social existence, has passed into the rank of a universally stigmatized injustice and tyranny.
>
> Mill 1944: 59

Mill cites slavery and discrimination on the basis of colour, race and sex as examples of practices once considered necessary for the public good that over time came to be seen as a denial of a right. An example from recent history is the right of women to equal pay.

This point is of particular relevance for advocacy. It means that, through advocating for a change in public opinion and attitude, disability services can move from being granted subject to resources, as at present, to being granted automatically as of right to ensure the disabled do not suffer injustice (see 'A Missed Opportunity to Advance Equal Rights', Frank Conaty, *Irish Times*, 29 April 2005).

At the same time the government recognises the need and entitlement people with disabilities have for services even if they are not granted automatically. In July 2006, the government launched major plans for improved disability services. The plans relate to the introduction of specific services in six areas and will be implemented by six government departments. The improved services will be in health, communications, environment, employment, social welfare and transport. Resources to implement the plans were said to be in place. (See Christine Newman's report, *Irish Times*, 26 July 2006.)

SEXUAL RIGHTS AND DISABILITY

People with disabilities have a right to sexual expression and to form loving sexual relationships the same as any other person. It is an important right because sexuality is central to a sense of self, and a healthy relationship to sexuality is necessary for well-being. This is an issue on which there is still a need to change the perception that denies or discourages sexuality for disabled people for the mistaken reason that it is somehow inappropriate or from over-protection. Families and others who care for people with disabilities may need training in under-standing and supporting disabled people's sexual needs, development and behaviour. In practice, disabled people's right to express their sexuality means they have a right to support. This includes relationship and sexuality education to enable them to make informed choices as far as is possible, as well as providing them with opportunities to socialise. It also includes practical support for couples who wish to marry and live independently. In the case of those who have learning challenges, there are understandable protective concerns relating to emotional vulnerability and willing consent, and there are risks of exploitation and abuse. However, without minimising the difficulties there may be in particular cases, with proper safeguards and supports it should be possible for many people with disabilities who want to enjoy their right to a fulfilling sexual life to do so safely.

CONFLICTS OF RIGHTS

Difficulty arises when there is conflict between two or more rights. For example, in child protection, a child's right to safety and security can be in conflict with the right of parents to care for their children. Here the child's best interest is always given priority. Care teams can face difficulties in particular cases in deciding what course of action is in the child's best interest.

Abortion and euthanasia are two issues which can be represented in terms of a conflict of rights. A number of moral arguments are advanced on each side of these issues. The following is a brief summary of the general position. For a more detailed account of some of the arguments made on both sides, see the articles in the abortion and euthanasia sections in *Ethics in Practice: An Anthology* (Hugh LaFollette (ed.), 2002). In the Introduction to the sections the editor provides a useful summary of the arguments made in the articles.

Abortion

The issue can be represented as a conflict between the right claimed on behalf of the unborn to life and a woman's right to freedom of choice to have her pregnancy ended in circumstances where it presents a crisis for her.

On the side of the right to life, the arguments are made that life is a continuous process from fertilisation and that all the genetic material that constitutes an individual is in place. On the side of a right to choose, the arguments are made that before a certain stage the foetus has not developed to a degree that constitutes the life of a person. It is also argued that the individual right to freedom includes a woman having a right to control what happens in and to her own body, and to her physical and emotional health where it is adversely affected by a crisis pregnancy. Central to the morality and legality of the issue is the differences in viewpoint people take on the question of when *life* becomes the *life of a person* and therefore entitled to the protection of the law. Some take the view that this occurs from conception, others that it occurs at implantation stage and others again that it does not occur before further stages in the development of the embryo and foetus have been reached. Acceptance that there are different viewpoints is one reason behind allowing for legal abortions before a certain stage in pregnancy. For example, disagreement among experts as to when unborn life constitutes the life of a person was central to the US Supreme Court's judgment in the landmark *Roe v. Wade* in 1973 which allowed for abortion. The Court also held that the US Constitution includes a concept of personal liberty or privacy that allows for choice.

In Ireland, an amendment to the Constitution in 1983 guarantees the right to life of the unborn with due regard to the equal right to life of the mother. Case X related to a fourteen-year-old girl who had been made pregnant by rape and was in danger of taking her own life from the trauma. In a landmark judgment in 1992, the Supreme Court ruled in the case that where there is a real and substantial risk to the life of a mother from her pregnancy, including from a risk of suicide, a risk that cannot be averted except by having an abortion, then abortion is in accordance with the Constitution. In case C in 1997, the High Court gave permission to the Eastern Health Board to assist a thirteen-year-old girl from the Travelling community, who was the subject of a care order and who had become pregnant from rape, to have an abortion in England on the grounds that she was suicidal as a result of becoming pregnant.

Proposed amendments to the Constitution to reverse or *roll back* the case X judgment were defeated in referenda in 1992 and in 2002. Factors facing the Irish government in trying to establish a position on the issue in the Constitution include the difficulty of finding an acceptable legal form of wording. Social policy is particularly aimed at reducing the number of crisis pregnancies, for which purpose the Crisis Pregnancy Agency was set up in 2001.

Euthanasia

Euthanasia is the ending of a person's life for them and on their behalf, where they are suffering from an incurable illness or condition which they find they can no longer bear. The illness or condition may either be considered terminal, as in a case of a person with a particular form of cancer, or not terminal, as in a case of a person with paraplegia. Euthanasia can either be voluntary, where it is requested by a patient, or involuntary, where a patient is not in a position to make his/her wishes known because of incapacity, such as deep persistent coma (termed a vegetative state), and euthanasia is sought on his/her behalf by the next of kin. Doctor-assisted suicide is related to euthanasia. This is where a doctor supplies a patient with the means to end his/her own life. Euthanasia and doctor-assisted suicide are illegal in Ireland and most other countries. Holland and Belgium are two EU countries in which euthanasia is legal under certain conditions and with safeguards.

A number of moral arguments are made to support the idea of euthanasia as a right. They include the argument from personal autonomy. Since we make choices about how we live we should have a right to choose how we die. It is also argued that people have a right to relieve their suffering and to die with dignity. However, there are a number of arguments against euthanasia as a right. One is that society has a right to ensure that life is respected and valued in everyone's interest and that this would be diminished if euthanasia is allowed. Another argument is that society has the right to protect its citizens, and if there was a legal right to euthanasia, vulnerable people may choose it either for mistaken reasons or under pressure. It is also said to go against nature.

A particular issue arises in relation to the right of people to have their life ended for them after they have been in a vegetative state for a period of years with little prospect of recovery. In a landmark *Ward of Court* case in Ireland in 1994, the Supreme Court ruled on appeal that a feeding tube which had kept a woman alive in a near-vegetative state for over twenty years could be removed. A mother took the case to court on her daughter's behalf. The Court ruled that there is a right to die naturally and that the woman's underlying condition would be the legal cause of her death and not the removal of the feeding tube. In this way it was argued not to be a case of involuntary euthanasia and not to be setting a precedent for it.

Rights of Separated Children Seeking Asylum Who Are in State Care

The Ombudsman for Children, Emily Logan, yesterday told a UN committee in Geneva that the state's treatment of separated children seeking asylum was in breach of UN and European conventions on children's rights.

In a submission Ms Logan said the vast majority of such children were accommodated in privately owned hostels, operated by staff without any childcare training, and did not meet the standards for residential centres where Irish children are placed.

'The inferior care provided to separated children seeking asylum is unacceptable and places the state in breach of its obligation to prevent discrimination under the UN Convention on the Rights of the Child and the European Convention on Human Rights,' she said.

(Source: Carl O'Brien, Social Affairs Correspondent, *Irish Times*, 8 June 2006)

CASE STUDY 5.1

A Right to Equal Status: Case Study of Treatment of Traveller Woman by a Local Authority

Consider points of human rights arising from the following case. A Traveller woman was living in substandard accommodation in a mobile home on a site which was constantly flooded. She applied for a house which she knew had been vacant for some time. Despite repeated requests, supported by social worker reports, the local authorities concerned did not allocate alternative housing. Following correspondence between the Equality Authority and the local authorities, the complainant was offered the house for which she had applied. The case came under the Equal Status Act.

(Source: Carol Coulter, *Irish Times*, 26 July 2005, from the Equality Authority's Annual Report for 2004)

Exercise 5.1

Check out Amnesty International's website and/or literature for examples of documented human rights abuses. Select one example and, drawing from your understanding of human rights, explain why the abuse is morally wrong.

CRITICAL EVALUATION

Difficulty Proving Rights Exist: Existence Not Self-evident

A crucial point about rights is the claim that they can be proven to exist from self-evidence. Aquinas's *proof* for the existence of natural laws amounts to a claim that it is self-evident to our reason that such laws do exist when we reflect on the fact that all human beings have basic inclinations. It remains the general understanding that rights are justified from self-evidence arising from the recognition that we do have natural tendencies in common – whether we want to regard them as giving rise to natural laws or not. But are rights self-evident?

Some would argue that they are. They argue that it is self-evident to reason that humans have certain basic tendencies in common and that rights come from this, especially equality rights. It can be argued, for example, that from natural tendencies to self-preservation, to have children and to live in society come the equal rights of all children to protection and development. On this basis a child, for example, who becomes homeless is not having her/his rights upheld.

The American Declaration of Independence also claims that rights are self-evidently true. It famously states, 'We hold these truths to be self-evident, that all men are created equal, that they are endowed by their Creator with certain unalienable Rights, that among these are Life, Liberty and the pursuit of Happiness'. In a similar vein the French Declaration of the Rights of Man and of the Citizen refers to 'natural, inalienable and sacred Rights of Man' (cited in d'Entreves 1964: 48).

However, for some philosophers natural rights are not self-evident. Vardy and Grosh (1999: 198) make the point that if natural rights existed 'it would be as if each infant were born with an indelible stamp on his or her forehead indicating the list of rights which must not, in any circumstances, be interfered with because they were implanted there by Nature.' Clearly this is not the case. There is not the same physical or empirical evidence (i.e. evidence from any of the five senses) for natural rights as there is for the brain and heart we are born with. Rights in this sense are not self-evident.

In addition, if rights were self-evident, then you would expect they would be readily respected. However, the actual behaviour of people and governments throughout history down to the present day has often flown in the face of a recognition that human beings have natural rights. This is cited as evidence that there are no such things as human rights, or at least that if there are such rights that they are far from being self-evident from nature. d'Entreves (1964: 74) makes this point when he says that the history of human behaviour is 'the stumbling block of all natural law theories' and, as we have seen, the main philosophical source for the existence of rights is natural law. However, you could argue that violations of human rights don't disprove the existence of human rights as derived from natural law theory. All that the violations show is how weak and imperfect human beings are morally.

Nevertheless, the reason of lack of self-evidence for the natural existence of rights led Bentham to dismiss the notion of natural rights as 'nonsense' and the notion of absolute natural rights as 'nonsense on stilts' (cited by Almond 2004: 266). Also, for MacIntyre 'there are no self-evident truths', and 'natural and human rights then are fictions' (1985: 69–70).

Neither Bentham nor MacIntyre are arguing against the spirit of human rights. As we will see in later chapters, there is a strong social care element in their ethics. All they are arguing is that the idea of rights is not a philosophically justifiable way of understanding why people should be provided with social care.

It can also be argued that Kant's ethics does not provide a basis for human rights. This is basically because Kant accepts that in practice our behaviour is caused, and so he has great difficulty showing how we can have free will at the same time. If free will cannot be shown to exist, then it removes one way of understanding why everyone has the same moral status and why they should be treated as having equal rights. This criticism is explained in more detail in Chapter 7, where we will consider some of the reasons why people may not be in control of their actions as one way of understanding why having empathy is a value.

Legal Acceptance of Some Rights

Despite the difficulty of proving that rights naturally exist, there is a definite sense in which rights *do exist* – this is as part of international agreements and covenants (Vardy and Grosch: 199). Here they are known as human rights, and the reference to them as 'natural' is dropped. Almond also makes this point (2004: 261) when she says, 'The practical discussions of rights . . . are likely to involve what are today called human rights. The justification of rights of this sort is essentially ethical, although the international community, in attempting to enshrine them in law, seeks to convert their justification into a matter of fact and practice.' It is for this reason that instead of reference to 'rights', the phrase *legally protected interests* is sometimes used.

Does Lack of Proof Matter?

Does it matter if it can't be proved that each person has certain human rights? Can we not just take it that it is highly desirable to look on people as having rights? Well, of course we can. However, the point is that the lack of a clear and universally accepted theoretical justification for human rights may be seen as making it easier for people and governments not to provide for rights in practice. The problem is that if human rights in practice are viewed only as a product of agreement, then the level of moral compulsion that agreements can afford is not as strong as it would be if rights could be proved to exist morally. If there is no other authority for rights besides the agreement, there is nothing else to stop a person or government from failing to provide for this agreement, or breaking the agreement when it suits them and they feel they can get away with it. This is a point made by Buckle (2004: 168). It is the same criticism that is made of social contract theories of morality, which we will look at in Chapter 10.

REVIEW

The idea that people have rights has proved an effective moral justification for bringing about social and political improvements. There is a philosophical difficulty proving that people actually do have rights. The claim that it is self-evident that people have rights from the existence of common natural tendencies is open to challenge. However, rights have become incorporated into international agreements and domestic law. Whether viewed as rights or legally protected interests, they can provide legal force for provision of certain welfare services. At the same time, services do not have to be provided automatically in full unless there is specific legal requirement to do so, but under international agreements they must be progressively realised.

FURTHER READING

Banks, S. (2006) *Ethics and Values in Social Work*, 3rd ed., Palgrave Macmillan (check Chapter 5).

Conaty, F. (2005) 'A Missed Opportunity to Advance Equal Rights', *Irish Times*, 29 April.

Vardy, P. and Grosh, P. (1999) *The Puzzle of Ethics*, HarperCollins (Chapter 16).

For information on equality, see the Equality Authority's website at www.equality.ie.

REFERENCES

Almond, B. (2004) 'Rights' in *A Companion to Ethics*, P. Singer (ed.), Blackwell.

Aquinas, Saint Thomas (1998) *On Law, Morality and Politics*, W. Baumgarth and R. Regan SJ (eds.), Hackett.

Buckle, S. (2004) 'Natural Law' in *A Companion to Ethics*, P. Singer (ed.), Blackwell.

Copleston, F. (1957) *Aquinas*, Pelican Books.

d'Entreves, A. (1964) *Natural Law: An Introduction to Legal Philosophy*, Hutcheson University Library.

Dinan, D. (2005) *Ever Closer Union: An Introduction to European Integration*, Palgrave Macmillan.

LaFollette, H. (ed.) (2002) *Ethics in Practice: An Anthology*, Blackwell (the articles on 'Abortion' and 'Euthanasia').

Mill, J. (1944) *Utilitarianism, Liberty and Representative Government*, Everyman's Library.

Norman, R. (1998) *The Moral Philosophers: An Introduction to Ethics*, 2nd ed., Oxford University Press. ('Rights-Based Ethics' pp. 185–189).

Quinn, G. (2004) cited in *Irish Times*, 10 December.

Note: The rights agreements and laws referred to can be accessed on the internet by keying in the relevant title.

6
The Greatest Happiness Principle

OVERALL AIM

To explore an influential principle which claims to show that the happiness of everyone is equally important.

LEARNING OUTCOMES

At the end of this chapter you should be able to:

- Explain the basis of the greatest happiness principle in the idea of equality and desire for happiness.
- Describe happiness in terms of avoiding pain and increasing pleasure.
- Explain how happiness is estimated in ethical decision-making.
- Appreciate the role the principle played in the introduction and development of the welfare state.
- Draw from the principle to support reducing hardship by meeting welfare needs.
- Draw from the principle as a guide in providing care in group settings.
- Demonstrate understanding for some of the main criticisms of the principle.

INTRODUCTION

Not everyone does well in society. Some people are said to 'lose out' or to 'get left behind' in relation to their standard of living. They experience unhappiness or misery from poverty. In caring for clients, care workers will frequently come across cases where poverty is a big factor in the reasons why clients need care. They may need direct help with food, clothing, bill payments or housing. The state provides a range of welfare services for those requiring help, e.g. jobseekers' supports, family income supplement and back-to-school clothing and footwear allowance. Also, voluntary agencies such as St Vincent de Paul and the Simon Community provide direct help with basic needs. In some cases clients may not be aware of their legal entitlements to welfare services and care workers can play an important role in helping them to obtain a service.

Figures compiled by the Department of Health and Children and the Health Service Executive (HSE) show that the number of children in the care of the state has been increasing significantly to just over 5,000 in 2004. A minority are taken into care for reasons of physical or sexual abuse. For the majority, the causes relate to neglect due to poverty or parents' inability to cope. Also, official figures show that the number of children who are homeless increased to almost 500 in 2004 (Carl O'Brien, *Irish Times*, 15 and 29 August 2006). More help from family support services, especially in early stages of family difficulty, is seen as the best way of helping to reduce the need for children to be taken into state care or for them to become homeless.

Poverty in particular is seen as a contributory factor behind a range of social problems. It is linked to child neglect, addiction, substance abuse and domestic violence. Child poverty is a particular care need in Ireland. It is linked to a range of problems which children can go on to experience, such as educational underachievement, welfare dependency and crime.

People who suffer from consistent poverty are said to live in households having an income of less than 60 per cent of the country's median or middle point along with experiencing any one of eight deprivation factors. These are:

- Being unable to afford a substantial meal on at least one day in the previous two weeks.
- Going without heating at some stage in the previous year.
- Having debt problems arising from ordinary living expenses.
- Being unable to afford two pairs of strong shoes, or a roast once a week, or a meal with meat, chicken or fish every second day, or new (not second-hand) clothes or a warm, waterproof coat.

People *at risk* of poverty are categorised as having income of less than 60 per cent of the median or middle point, without experiencing deprivation factors (also known as relative poverty). In Ireland, the level of consistent poverty has remained largely unchanged in recent years – while the number at risk of poverty dropped slightly between 2004 and 2005. There is a significant amount of what is called 'hidden' poverty. This includes poverty among what is called 'the working poor', i.e. people on low incomes who are also usually outside the income limits for entitlement to state benefits (Carl O'Brien, *Irish Times*, 12 August and 22 December 2006).

2005 Poverty Statistics for Ireland

7 per cent of the population experience consistent poverty.
18·5 per cent of the population are said to be 'at risk' of poverty.

Groups identified as most vulnerable to experiencing poverty are:

- lone-parent households
- the ill or the disabled
- the unemployed
- people living alone and the elderly.

Over one third of persons in consistent poverty are children under sixteen. And one in ten of all children under fourteen are affected by it.

(Source: EU Survey of Income and Living Conditions 2005 (EU–SILC) available at www.socialinclusion.ie)

The greatest happiness principle relates to providing happiness for the greatest possible number in society, and it views the happiness of everyone as equally important. This makes it a particularly relevant ethical principle for supporting the happiness needs of those who experience hardship, particularly from poverty. The theory that provides for the greatest happiness is known as utilitarianism.

UTILITARIANISM

Two Basic Features

The utilitarian view is based on accepting that there is:

- A basic equality and freedom of all citizens in a democratic society.
- A desire for happiness on the part of each person.

Since all are equal and have an equal right to happiness, Mill claims that it follows from this that everyone should be catered for as much as possible. He believes that 'society between equals can only exist on the understanding that the interests of all are to be regarded equally' (Mill 1944: 29). In addition, Mill claims that being concerned about the happiness of others (altruism) is its own good and has its own benefit.

Altruism is Part of Human Nature

He speaks of 'the desire to be in unity with our fellow creatures, which is already a powerful principle in human nature'. He adds that 'the social state' is 'natural', 'necessary' and 'habitual' (29). This is a view similar to Aristotle's – that human nature is essentially social.

Altruism is Pleasurable

We can learn from experience that caring for others is a pleasure. Mill refers to people who are lucky enough to be able to satisfy their own pleasures to the extent they desire, but who remain dissatisfied. He says the reason they remain dissatisfied is because if they are caring for nobody but themselves, they miss out on one pleasure essential for anyone's happiness, which is the pleasure that comes from acting in the interests of others (13).

Altruism Proves Itself in Practice as the Meaning of Ethics

Mill appeals to the psychological facts of experience when he holds that the more we have a society working on the basis of people co-operating to provide for the interests of each other, the more this will become confirmed in people's minds as the overall meaning of ethics (30).

The Principle Itself

Utilitarianism combines and gives expression to the two features of equality and desire for happiness in one overall principle. This principle was put forward by the founder of utilitarianism, Jeremy Bentham (1748–1832). It is the principle that the good is that which provides for the greatest happiness of the greatest number of people. He named it in short 'the Greatest Happiness Principle'.

This principle provides a criterion for judging actions. The criterion is that an action is good as far as it produces more happiness than unhappiness for the greatest number of people and it is bad as far as it produces more unhappiness or misery than happiness.

Mill (1806–73) begins his essay 'Utilitarianism' by stating the basic principle laid down by Bentham: 'The creed which accepts as the foundation of morals, Utility, or the Greatest Happiness Principle, holds that actions are right in proportion as they tend to promote happiness, wrong as they tend to produce the reverse of happiness' (4).

Meaning of Happiness: Pleasure or Utility

But what is happiness? The first thing to strike anyone about the question is that happiness can mean different things to different people. We have seen how it means *flourishing* for Aristotle. Bentham, however, takes a basic, practical view of the meaning of happiness to try to ensure it accommodates everyone's view. To start with, like Aristotle, he regards happiness as what everyone desires. At the most basic level, he says we desire to avoid pain and increase our pleasure. In addition, Bentham did not make any distinction in quality between what gives people pleasure. It's a matter of whatever appeals to the individual.

Mill agrees with Bentham in identifying happiness with pleasure. 'By happiness is meant intended pleasure, and the absence of pain; by unhappiness pain and the privation of pleasure'(4). We desire things for our happiness, either because they give us pleasure or they are a means to obtaining pleasure. We avoid them because they cause us pain or are a means of avoiding pain (6). Pleasure is understood in both its physical and emotional senses. *Satisfaction preference* is a broader term some utilitarians use today to identify what all people desire.

Higher Pleasures

For Mill, what gives us pleasure is not confined to the satisfaction of our bodily desires for good food, wine or sex. He provides what he sees as a more refined understanding in claiming that some activities enable us to enjoy higher pleasures. 'Human beings have faculties more elevated than the animal appetites, and when once made conscious of them, do not regard anything as happiness which does not include their gratification' (7). Higher pleasures include enjoyment of music or nature or company.

Mill is sometimes accused of being high-minded in claiming that pleasures of the intellect or spirit are higher than those of the bodily senses, but he says it is simply a fact of human experience that people find such pleasures indispensable to their happiness once they get to know them. It is 'an unquestionable fact that those who are equally acquainted with, and equally capable of appreciating and enjoying, both, do give a most marked preference to the manner of existence which employs the higher faculties' (8). So, he is not imposing a high-minded view of pleasure by having recourse to some moral authority such as human reason – he is not trying to lecture us on what is good for us. Instead he is leaving it up to people to decide from their own experience the kind of things that give them pleasure and constitute their happiness. People themselves are 'the only competent judges'. There is 'no other tribunal to be referred to' (10).

The Equal Happiness of All

The key point of utilitarian ethics is that judgments about good and bad or right and wrong relate not just to my own preference for happiness, but to the preferences of others who may be affected. The theory requires us to treat our own happiness as no more important (but no less either) than their happiness. This means that in making judgments about how best to behave, we must regard ourselves 'as strictly impartial as a disinterested and benevolent spectator' (16).

However, as individuals in our ordinary daily affairs, we can't literally take everybody's happiness into account – this is beyond our capacity. Realistically, we can take into account only the happiness of those few with whom we are involved, but in doing so we are playing our part in contributing to the greatest happiness of the greatest number. Those, however, who engage in forming public policy and making the law are in a position to take decisions for the happiness of everybody. Therefore, they should always take into account the preferences not just of some, but of all (17–18). If this can be done by reducing the great misery of a few at little cost to everyone else, then this is the morally right policy. In the next section we will try to make clear why this is required by the principle.

Not Necessarily Majority Preference

A utilitarian is not saying that right and wrong depends solely on what the majority see as their happiness. It is not a matter of *counting heads* or simple democracy. The greatest happiness principle has sometimes been misinterpreted in this way. The principle requires us to produce the *greatest happiness* of the greatest number. This means that if a particular decision produces a larger amount of happiness for a minority (say through relief of misery) compared to a small reduction in happiness for the majority, then that decision is justified if it produces the greatest happiness overall. In making a decision, all the amounts of happiness produced for individuals have to be added together (aggregated) and set against the amount of loss in happiness others may experience from the decision to see which is the biggest, the increase or loss in happiness. If there is a bigger loss in happiness than there is a production of it, then the decision is wrong. But if there is a bigger production of happiness overall than a loss, then the decision is morally right. For example, if instead of spending money on a new state-of-the-art sports stadium, which would bring some happiness to a lot of people, the government could bring more overall happiness by using the money to provide a care service such as long-term accommodation for the homeless, then using the money for the care service is the morally correct decision even though it would benefit relatively few people. Once the benefit to the minority results in the greatest overall amount of happiness, then it is justified.

Estimating Consequences: Giving Weight to Subjective Factors

For Mill, as we have seen, pleasures differ not just in quantity but also in quality. This means there is a huge difficulty in being able to measure the quality of one pleasure with another. The same problem arises in measuring the extent of hardship people suffer due to their particular conditions. To be able to accurately measure pleasure and hardship, we would need to be able to isolate people's subjective experience of them in relation to some highly variable factors, such as intensity and duration. It is simply not possible. Thus, for Mill, instead of any actual measurement, all we can do is come up with our best estimate. This is done by considering the consequences our decision will have for ourselves and others.

Consequentialism

If the consequences of our decision to act in a certain way, *in so far as we can know those consequences*, produce more happiness over unhappiness, then the action is morally right. If the consequences produce more unhappiness, then the action is morally wrong. The only relevant factor in making the estimation is consequences (18). For this reason, utilitarian theory is often called 'consequentialism'. Phrases that express the consequentialist approach to ethics include 'for the greater good' and when we advise against an action because it will do 'more harm than good'.

Steps in Estimating Consequences

To try and estimate consequences of an action in terms of the pleasure or harm it will bring for people is difficult. If it's to be done accurately and thoroughly, we may often need to:

1. Map out the different courses of action which we could decide on as a response to an issue or problem.
2. Estimate the consequences each course will have for all concerned, and link those consequences to our estimation of people's references and the extent to which they will bring them pleasure or pain.
3. Treat everyone's preference for pleasure or happiness, our own included, as of equal value.

Rule and Act Utilitarians

As a help in estimating which consequences will generally produce the most happiness, some utilitarians believe we should follow rules. Rule utilitarians claim that we should not decide on which *particular* act is the best, but which *type* of act, if done by most people, would produce the greatest happiness of the greatest number. They advocate sticking to certain rules as the best way of achieving the happiness of everybody. They say we can learn what these rules should be from experience of the type of actions that tend to cause unhappiness or happiness. For example, they argue that there should be a rule requiring everybody to tell the truth and not tell lies because experience tells us that lying generally causes more unhappiness than happiness. Mill is a rule utilitarianist. However, he does not believe in following rules at any cost. He recognises that the complicated nature of human affairs will always throw up justifiable exceptions to the rules (20–21). Mill's allowance for exceptions is quoted in the critical evaluation of Kant's ethics in Chapter 4.

Act utilitarians, on the other hand, hold that each act has to be examined on its own merits. In other words, we have to keep an open mind and not decide in advance on which act will produce the greatest happiness of the greatest number. Moral decisions have to be made on a case-by-case basis. For example, an act utilitarian would say that we should be truthful and honest about a particular matter only if it can be shown that this brings more happiness to all concerned than unhappiness.

THE GREATEST HAPPINESS PRINCIPLE AND SOCIAL CARE

Inclusion of Others on an Equal Basis

Utilitarianism is directly related to social care since it requires people to be concerned with the happiness of others at least as much as with their own happiness. In addition, utilitarians recognise that since governments are in a position to make decisions affecting the happiness of everyone, social policies have a key role to play in providing for the happiness of everyone where everyone is treated as having an equal desire for happiness.

Guide for Decision-making in Casework

Situations frequently arise in care work where the behaviour of a client is having a negative effect on other clients in care. As a result, care teams have to make hard decisions about the happiness of both the particular client and the other clients. Estimating the greatest happiness produced overall by a particular decision can be *one way* they could morally justify a particular decision. Here it is important to emphasise again that giving priority to an individual client who has particular needs may produce the greatest happiness overall – on the other hand, it may not. This is what has to be estimated and a judgment made.

Gives Priority to Reducing Suffering

In general, the theory regards relief of suffering as the main way in which the most happiness can be provided overall. In other words, it takes the view that more happiness is likely to come from relief of suffering than from providing additional pleasure to those who are not suffering.

Social Policy Influence

In devising his utilitarian theory, Bentham was motivated by the need for social reform to end poverty. In particular, he wanted to end the position in which the wealthy and powerful in British society at the time enjoyed privileges which gave them an advantage over everybody else. His aim was to provide an overall ethical principle to guide political decision-making, especially in the way that those decisions are enshrined in law.

For Mill, too, deprivation of one kind or another was the only real obstacle in the way of bringing about happiness for almost everybody (12). He believed that 'all the grand courses, in short, of human suffering are in a great degree, many of them almost entirely, conquerable by human care and effort' (14).

Education to Empower Citizens to Make Informed Choices

In particular, Mill saw a need for education. Through education, people can also come to realise what is of value or worth for their happiness or pleasure. He especially believed that education would enable people to appreciate the higher pleasures that contribute most to a happy life. Through education, people can also come to realise better how their own interest is bound up with the interest of others. Education, too, he believed, is central to developing in people a sense of individual freedom, which for him is a core value. The realisation of personal freedom is necessary to ensure that people can determine their own lives and not have authority imposed on them. His classic essay, *On Liberty*, is one of the foundational pieces of writing in support of liberalism.

CASE STUDY 6.1

Case Studies: Individual Behaviour in Group Care Settings

Having regard to the greatest happiness principle, consider the response of a care team to provide appropriate care to overcome the difficulties in caring for both the individual and the group in the following examples. For example, what might be the consequences of excluding the individual from participating in the group in the short term? What might be the consequences of allowing the individual to remain? If your view of the appropriate decision includes a need for more resources or services, consider how the greatest happiness principle might support their provision. To consider more particular examples of the general ones mentioned below, include details relating to a possible client and his/her background.

1. A hyperactive child in a child care setting who appears to have strong attention-seeking needs.
2. An autistic adolescent in a group care setting whose behaviour is disrupting care activities for other clients.
3. A seriously troubled youth in a secure detention centre.
4. A homeless man who persistently breaks house rules in a centre for the homeless by drinking alcohol on the premises and becoming boisterous.

Exercise 6.1

Question for Consideration and Discussion: Means and Ends

Does the end always justify the means where the end succeeds in providing the greatest happiness of the greatest number? Can you think of examples where you can argue that it does not justify the means because the means go against other values that are more important than the greatest happiness of the greatest number?

Exercise 6.2

Question for Consideration and Discussion: Increasing Overseas Aid

In the light of the greatest happiness principle, consider and discuss whether or not Ireland should increase its overseas aid with reference to the position outlined below, and with reference to Ireland's increasing prosperity over the period involved.

In the year 2000, while addressing the United Nations Millennium Summit in New York, the Taoiseach made a promise on behalf of the Irish people that Ireland would increase its overseas development aid budget to 0·7 per cent of GNP (Gross National Product) by 2007. The level recommended by the UN is 0·7 per cent, and has been already met by five countries. In meeting this target Ireland would be helping to set an example for other countries to follow – we would be sending a strong signal regarding how seriously we took our obligation to care for the world's poorest people. However, a few years later, the government announced that it would not now be meeting that target and it would now be achieved more gradually by 2012. The rate for 2007 is 0·5 per cent. One of the reasons the government gave was that it could not afford the increase in the light of spending requirements to meet domestic needs. The Tánaiste explained in the Dáil that the UN pledge had been dropped because of competing domestic demands. She said, 'Unfortunately, there are many competing demands, particularly in the area of disability in which the government has had to deliver significant increases in funding.' (Source: *Irish Times*, 25 November 2004)

CRITICAL EVALUATION

Provides an Ethics Inclusive of People's Preferences

Under the greatest happiness principle, morality is not imposed. It is a matter for individuals to decide what is good and bad for their happiness. The theory respects the authority of each person to know his own best interest. It then provides for decision-making based on trying to accommodate everyone's best interest as far as possible.

Difficulty Estimating Consequences

There is difficulty in having accurate knowledge of what people prefer for their happiness as a basis for making good ethical decisions. Also, there is difficulty accurately estimating the amount of happiness an action will produce overall. The problem is compounded when short-term and long-term consequences have to be included in the estimation.

Also, since estimating the amount and quality of pleasure has to take into account everyone's preferences, there is no reason *in itself* for giving priority to relieving poverty. For example, suppose you could show that more happiness would in fact be produced for more people by building a sports stadium than by using the same money to provide long-term accommodation for the homeless – this would then indicate a moral requirement to use the money for the stadium. The spirit of utilitarianism is directed toward relieving misery in society as a priority, but unless this can be shown to produce the most happiness overall in a particular action, then there is no moral justification for doing so.

Difficult Not to Give Priority to Own Happiness

Another difficulty with utilitarianism is that it underestimates the priority people feel they are entitled to give to their own happiness. For example, it would seem that if a disabled person's desire for independent living causes more unhappiness for his family than the happiness it would bring him/her, then s/he has to bow to the interests of his/her family as the morally right response. The same would apply in the case of a person who wants a divorce.

In his essay 'Famine, Affluence and Morality', utilitarian philosopher Peter Singer gives a striking example of the principle that we must regard the general happiness as overruling our own desires where the two are in conflict. Singer argues that because our happiness counts no more than other people's happiness, and because world hunger is a condition of extreme misery, then people in the affluent Western world are morally obliged to do whatever it takes (including, if necessary, drastically reducing their standard of living) in order to provide for the greatest happiness of the greatest number.

But it appears to go against a natural intuition to say that our own happiness counts for no more than the happiness of others. It is said to be 'counter-intuitive'. Certainly, in practice, people generally have always felt they have a natural right to give priority to their own happiness.

No Allowance for a Distinction between Acting and Omitting to Act

Since the happiness of all is the sole criterion, the theory also claims that we are just as responsible for the harm we can prevent (if we don't do anything to relieve it when we could do so) as we are for the harm that we directly cause. Utilitarians don't make a distinction between omitting to act and acting when it comes to having moral responsibility. However, most people would say that while we may have *some* responsibility to act to prevent others experiencing harm, such as famine victims, it is not the same responsibility we would have if we actually caused the harm.

On the other hand, regarding the question of moral responsibility to end poverty in developing countries, one of the arguments made is that policies of developed countries on trade, debt repayments and arms sales contribute directly to causing poverty-related harm. On this issue, some argue strongly that developed countries have at least some direct responsibility both to end existing poverty in under-developed countries and to change their policies so that they don't contribute to causing harm.

No Allowance for Motive or Intention as Morally Relevant Factor

A further criticism made is that utilitarianism excludes motive or intention in assessing the morality of an action. Assessment is based solely on consequences. Yet in law, for example, intention is taken into account. It matters significantly if the killing of another person was intended, for then it is murder, whereas if it was unintended it is manslaughter. If a care team's decision to place a client in foster care produces more unhappiness than happiness for the client and foster parents, it is clearly relevant to assessing the action morally that it was the care team's intention to produce happiness.

Assumes the Good Equals the Greatest Happiness

Mill accepts that he has not proved by logic that the greatest happiness principle is true – he says that he cannot. Any theory, he believes, has to start by assuming its first principle is true, and utilitarianism is no different (32). Nevertheless, he argues that the basis of utilitarianism is 'psychologically true' and that is all the proof that is needed (36). He explains this as shown below.

> No reason can be given why the general happiness is desirable, except that each person, so far as he believes it to be attainable, desires his own happiness. This, however, being a fact, we have not only all the proof which the case admits of, but all which it is possible to require, that happiness is a good: that each person's happiness is a good to that person, and the general happiness, therefore, a good to the aggregate of all persons.
>
> Mill 1944: 32–3

Benn points out that this view, which is the basis of utilitarianism, can be criticised. This is because it is claiming that, in one way or another, we always act to obtain pleasure for ourselves. But is this true? For Benn, the reason we get pleasure from obtaining what we want may not simply be because it satisfies our desires, but because we regard what we desire as having a fundamental value. For example, the pleasure we get from helping a friend is not just because it satisfies our desire, but because we recognise an independent value in friendship as something good in itself. As Benn puts it, 'The pleasure of getting what we want often comes because we attach an independent value to the things that we want, and manage to get' (Benn 1988: 69). Mill, though he does not seem to realise it, implicitly attaches an independent value to the higher pleasures. He is strongly implying that they are good, not just because we desire them once we have experience of them, but that there is something good about them regardless of whether we desire them or not.

REVIEW

The greatest happiness principle is a simple, practical response to the problem of understanding what good should mean. It is also supportive of social care in its view that everyone's desire for happiness is of equal value and should be provided for as much as possible. Even though it can be criticised on many grounds, it is a common sense view of ethics. In addition, it's likely that in practice it is the view of ethics that many people accept, at least in part, whether they are explicitly aware of doing so or not. This is because the consequences of our actions for others are a major factor in our view of what we consider to be the right thing to do.

FURTHER READING

Banks, S. (2006) *Ethics and Values in Social Work*, 3rd ed., Palgrave Macmillan (section on 'Utilitarian Principles' in Chapter 2).
Benn, P. (1998) *Ethics*, UCL Press (Chapter 3).
Norman, R. (1998) *The Moral Philosophers: An Introduction to Ethics*, 2nd ed., Oxford University Press (Chapter 7).

REFERENCES

Benn, P. (1998) *Ethics*, UCL Press.
Mill, J. (1944) *Utilitarianism, Liberty and Representative Government*, Everyman's Library.
LaFollette, H. (ed.) (2002) *Ethics in Practice: An Anthology*, 2nd ed., Blackwell (Singer's essay 'Famine, Affluence and Morality').

7
Empathy

OVERALL AIM

To explore why having empathy for people in their need for care is understandable in terms of the restrictions they face in having the freedom to cope adequately with their lives.

LEARNING OUTCOMES

At the end of this chapter you should be able to:

- Distinguish between three senses of freedom: freedom as a challenge, freedom in relation to living circumstances and freedom of the will.
- Explain how difficulties coping with the challenge of freedom can give rise to understandable reasons why people may come in need of care.
- Explain the restrictive effect of poverty and incapacity on practical freedom.
- Appreciate the view that people may have no, or limited, free will from understanding Spinoza's view that all behaviour is caused.

INTRODUCTION

Empathy arises as a human response to people from becoming aware of their conditions and circumstances which cause them suffering or hardship. We empathise with people who suffer from hunger, for example, and hunger is a care issue in Ireland. The recognition that some children go to school hungry has led to the setting up of breakfast clubs in some schools. Empathy is different from sympathy. To have sympathy means to share in the feeling of suffering which others have as a result of their difficulty. Empathy, on the other hand, is a capacity to identify emotionally with others in what they are going through. Empathy is different again from pity. Pity means feeling sorry for others. Also, feeling pity can include looking down on others as inferior to oneself, and when it does so it is unjustified and inappropriate. Empathy involves feeling for others on the basis of knowledge of their circumstances. We know what it is like to face challenges, limitations and opportunities in being free. This is central to our sense of self. It enables us to know, and identify with, what it is like for other people to experience demands, restrictions and opportunities. For example, we know what it is like not to have enough money for what we want, so we can empathise with people whose lack of money is a factor in their need for care.

For care providers, having understanding for people in the difficulties and hardships they experience is central to their work. It includes, in particular, the capacity to be attentive and responsive to their needs. Drawing from the work of Blum and Vetlesen, Banks links a capacity to have empathy with a capacity to have moral perception. To have empathy with people means being able to see the features of their life that matter to them, and in particular features that are causing them some difficulty (Banks 2004: 169–70).

In this chapter we will look at some of the ways in which people's freedom is affected such that they experience difficulties which may result in a need for care. Also, in the light of restrictions people face in their experience of freedom, they are said not to be fully responsible for what happens to them or for what they can do for themselves. In this way, too, we can come to understand why empathy is justified as a value and why it supports providing care to help people overcome their difficulties.

Freedom as an Existential Challenge

We experience ourselves as free to try to have the kind of life we want. But deciding on the kind of life we want can be a challenge. This is because we don't have certainty that any choice we make will necessarily be the best one. Freedom, in other words, can be experienced as an existential challenge.

Some existentialists, notably Sartre in his early works, say that people find themselves born into a world that has no absolute meaning or value. While there is a range of cultural meaning and value available, and while we may (or may not) have adequate material and emotional support for our needs, the real challenge is to cope with our life in terms of finding fulfilling meaning and value. We recognise that we have freedom to choose what will have meaning and value for us, but have no guarantee that the choices we make will be good ones.

Sartre says that we become who we are through the choices we make. As he puts it, 'For human reality, to be is to choose oneself' (1995: 440). We make ourselves by our choices, large or small, from the career we follow to the recreation we enjoy. Through my choices 'I am more and more sculpting my figure in the world' (427). Because we are free and, at the same time, have to express ourselves in some way, how we do so produces who we are. It makes us who we are essentially (438).

However, as Sartre saw it, this presents a big challenge. This is because whatever we choose, whatever we desire, whatever we give our attention to, has no intrinsic worth or purpose. Its only worth or purpose comes from the meaning and value we choose to give to it, but our choice will always be quite subjective and a matter for ourselves. There is nothing definite and objective to guide our choice. Even though our choices may relate to our needs and interests, they will still ultimately be random in that they could have been different to the actual ones we made.

At the same time, Sartre saw us facing the challenge of having to choose in the full light of the recognition of being responsible for our freedom – he describes this as a daunting challenge. He points out that the tendency is for people to hide from their responsibility. This results in people leading false lives of 'bad faith' in which they bury their freedom to make their own responsible choice about how best to live in their social roles or in subservience to some established source of authority. If this description of the human condition is correct, then it provides a reason for having understanding for difficulties people face in coping with their lives. It provides one possible element of the underlying understanding of why people may become depressed, or homeless, or develop addictions. It may also be an element in the underlying cause of some suicides, and suicides among young male adults is a particular problem in Ireland. Immediate contributory causes may be seen to lie in drinking to excess or depression. However, difficulties coping with the existential challenge may be an element lying behind such causes.

Practical Restrictions on Freedom: Poverty

A second difficulty people face arises from the lack of freedom they experience in a practical sense. Poverty is an example of restriction in living conditions, while disability and old age are examples of restriction from incapacity. Nobody is free in the sense of having no practical limits on what they can do. People are always restricted to some extent by their economic and social conditions, but people who are poor are more severely restricted than those who are well-off.

At the extreme, people in developing countries who suffer from absolute poverty have almost no freedom because they are restricted to mere physical survival. For the same reason, in Ireland, consistent poverty also restricts freedom. This notion of restricted freedom is included in the Combat Poverty Agency's definition of poverty where it states that people who are living in poverty 'are often excluded and marginalised from participating in activities that are the norm for other people' (Glossary, Combat Poverty Agency website: www.cpa.ie/povertyinireland/glossary.htm).

For example, people who are poor may not be able to afford the same range and quality of food that most people take for granted, or take part in common leisure activities such as having a night out or a holiday. People in need of social care can have practical limitations on their freedom through, for example, lack of simple services such as a guide dog or home help. One other particular example where poverty restricts people is in participation in higher education. In Ireland, fewer students from low-income households attend third-level education, particularly the universities, in proportion to those from middle- and upper-income house-holds, and poverty is seen as a significant reason for the imbalance. (See ESRI report 'A Review of Entry into Higher Education in 2004', available on ESRI's website: www.esri.ie.)

Problem of Free Will and Determinism

A third limitation people face relates to being able to make a free choice or to have free will. While most people believe that we do have free will, free will is always exercised in the context of influences acting on it. As a result, as we shall see, philosophers differ in their view on whether these influences still allow for free will or whether they actually cause our responses. Factors that influence free will include the immediate factors involved in a situation where we have to make a choice. Deeper factors lie in our genetic make-up and in our psychological and social background. For example, it is accepted that a person's genes can predispose him/her to certain behaviour such as depression or violence. Also, psychologists and psychotherapists often point to unconscious forces motivating a person, for example, a lack of parental love in childhood influencing a person's actions by making it hard for him/her to form and maintain stable and loving adult relationships. Understanding that people may not be able to have control over their actions because they lack free will is one way of understanding the value of having empathy for him/her.

Free Will and Acting under Influences: The Libertarian, *Soft* and *Hard* Determinist Views

Basically, three different positions are held on the question of whether or not we have free will. These are:

- We have complete free will to decide how we want to behave (the libertarian view).
- Influences affect our choices, but we still have free will because we can be aware of these influences and decide to let one rather than another be the cause of our decision. (This is the 'soft' determinist view. It is the view that free will is compatible with influences affecting our choices.)
- All our actions are completely determined by influences; in other words, they are caused and we have no free will. (This is the 'hard' determinist view. It is the view that free will is incompatible with influences since those influences cause or dictate our choices.)

The Libertarian View

We feel ourselves to have free will when we are faced with making a choice, for example, to stay in for the evening or go out. We may waver in our choice, but this still appears to us as evidence that we have it in our power to decide one way or the other. We don't feel we *have to* act in one way or another. Instead, we feel we have it within our power to act in whatever way we choose.

The Soft Determinist View

This emphasises that we do not have free will without coming under *some* influence which inclines our choice one way more than another. So, I will choose to stay in because I'm feeling tired, or I will choose to go out because I'm feeling restless. However, I can also be feeling restless and eager to go out and yet still choose to stay in. When this happens we feel in particular that we have free will because we are acting against the pressure of an influence. While our choice is always made in the context of various factors influencing it, and while we can be heavily influenced by those factors, we are still able to make a free choice. It is up to us to choose from among them. In this way, our choice is both influenced and free.

The Hard Determinist View

Hard determinists argue that free will is an illusion. Our actions can be completely understood in the light of causes acting on us, causes ultimately beyond our control. The *hard* determinist argues that our choice is caused, not by us, but by whatever the factor is that gives rise to the choice. So, for example, if we decide to stay in, and do so because we want to save money for another social occasion, then this is the factor that caused our decision. Even if we stay in to try to prove that we can act against our desire and so have free will, this can be viewed as the factor causing our decision!

A *hard* determinist view is probably the one most people would identify with least. We feel we do have free will, even if we come under strong influences. However, we will look in particular at Spinoza's *hard* determinism. He identified a lack of free will as central to understanding people's behaviour and to understanding what they needed to do to still lead good lives. In addition, we don't have to agree with Spinoza's view in full to recognise that people can come under a lot pressure, often severe, which results in them behaving in ways not good for them or for others close to them. An example is a young, single parent from a *broken home* in which there was unemployment, poverty and alcoholism who resorts to drugs to try to alleviate his/her problems. We can understand that in his/her case there are strong factors contributing to, if not actually causing, his/her behaviour. Spinoza's theory, while it is a bit difficult, helps us to understand more than other theories how it is that our actions are influenced by such factors, over which we may have little or no control. It can also help care workers in understanding why clients may have difficulty following care plans devised for them.

SPINOZA'S *HARD* DETERMINIST VIEW

Spinoza accepts that we *think* we have free will. It is just that we are mistaken in thinking we have it. The reason we think we have it is because we are *aware* of what we want to do, but we ignore the fact that there are causes lying behind any choice we make (Spinoza 1995: 30–31). We can see clearly two options before us, and imagine ourselves free to opt for one or the other, but this is to ignore the causes that lie behind our option. As he explains, 'Men are mistaken in thinking themselves free; and this opinion depends on this alone, that they are conscious of their actions and ignorant of the causes by which they are determined' (64).

For Spinoza, anything that happens to us or anything that we do is caused. It is said to be *determined*. It always occurs as a result of some cause or, more completely, a chain of causes outside our power. We cannot behave otherwise than we actually do because our behaviour is backed up by a whole chain of causes that have led directly to it. For example, suppose you feel frustrated because, while being distracted by a colleague, you accidentally deleted from your computer a difficult report you had spent a lot of time working on. Adding to your frustration is the fact that your supervisor wants the report urgently for a case conference and you know from experience that s/he will not be happy to hear that your report will not be ready for him/her in time. Spinoza points out that a whole chain of causes has led to your difficulty and frustration. Immediate causes include whatever caused your colleague to distract you (perhaps an urge to tell you about her new boyfriend). In addition, there is a whole host of background causes reaching ever further back. They include the cause of the urgency for the report, the causes that have led to you caring for this particular client rather than another one, the causes that have led the client to be in need of care, and even what caused you to work in social care in the first place. In this way, a chain of causes lies behind what is happening to you.

The Power of Emotions to Cause Behaviour

So what causes our behaviour such that we have no free will? For Spinoza, our emotions are the immediate cause of our actions. In particular, they cause us to behave as we do rather than our choices. Our emotions are triggered by some occurrence or other that has affected them. Emotions are so powerful, he believes, that we are in 'servitude' to them from our lack of power to keep them in check (139).

Primary Emotions: Desire, Pleasure and Pain

To understand the full force and scope of our emotions, they have to be seen in relation to three *primary emotions*. These are desire, pleasure and pain (122; 124). For him, emotions include our basic desires for food, drink and sex, etc. We can readily recognise their force behind our actions. However, desire, pleasure and pain have to do with *all* the emotions which cause our actions and not just with satisfying our physical desires and avoiding physical suffering. How can this be? The following is an example of how the primary emotions of desire, pleasure and pain cause what seems to be a free choice.

Example: Deciding on Legal Action for a Care Service

A father imagines himself free to take a legal action against the state, or not take it, in order to get the best professional service for his autistic child. The father thinks he is considering two images that consist *only* of thoughts in his mind. But this is to overlook the fact that first and foremost the father is automatically *drawn emotionally* on the basis of primary emotions of desire, pleasure and pain toward or away from any image he envisages as the best way of caring for his son.

Let's say the father is a careful and thoughtful man. He weighs up all the pros and cons of taking legal action and not taking it. Ultimately his decision will not be caused by his rational consideration of the options. Instead, those considerations will have more or less weight depending on how they relate to his desire for his son's care and his own need to avoid emotional pain and achieve emotional satisfaction. The decision will be due to whichever emotional pull proves strongest in avoiding emotional pain and providing him with emotional satisfaction in meeting his desire. If he decides to take legal action, then this is the course that emotionally satisfies him. It will result from a mix of emotions in play in him, emotions of parental love as well as frustration and anger. It is these emotions that impact on his desire to provide his son with the care he needs, and these emotions that impact on his own need to reduce his emotional pain and thereby achieve some emotional satisfaction. The emotions that give him most satisfaction in relation to his desire win out, and in this case they are the ones that lead to taking legal action – they win out over other emotions of, say, resignation or worry about the financial cost of going to court. In this way, the option of taking legal action proves stronger in him on the basis of his experience of the primary emotions of desire, pleasure and pain. While he has thought carefully about the advantages and disadvantages of the two options, nevertheless the deciding movement for one option over another is due to his rational considerations taking on an emotional colour of a particular strength or intensity. Knowledge, in short, only leads to action from being under the influence of emotion (150).

In this way, for Spinoza, our actions are always under the influence of our emotions. The only way to avoid being under the sway of one emotion is by another emotion taking over. Only an emotion can overcome an emotion: 'An emotion can neither be hindered nor removed save by a contrary emotion and one stronger than the emotion which is checked' (146).

For Spinoza, then, we think we are free to choose from our awareness of the choice presented to us, but behind this choice lie causes, most immediately from the power of the emotion acting on us which is driven by the primary emotions of desire, pleasure and pain.

Emotional Complexity

Spinoza provides a detailed account of the emotions, defining and describing many of them. From his account, a picture emerges of people as emotionally complex given the range and difference of the emotions to which we are subjected. He makes much of the fact that we experience emotional pressure. He refers more than once to the human experience of 'being assailed by emotions' (159). He also refers to the common experience of emotional conflict where more than one emotion is acting on us at any one time and we experience them in opposition to each other. He speaks of people as 'harassed by contrary emotions' (87).

All this, he says, is a sign that people often do not really know what they want. He sees people as often confused about their desires, whereby 'a man is drawn in different directions and knows not whither to turn' (126). As for those who do not experience any particularly strong emotions, they are easy prey to being taken over by any one emotion that surfaces (88). They are prone to act on a whim or impulse in seeking to satisfy the primary emotions of desire, pleasure and pain.

These kinds of emotional experiences, which he believes are common, emphasise how much we are in the grip of emotional causes and lack freedom in relation to them. Perhaps you are familiar with the feeling of having *mixed emotions* such as divided loyalty, or both anger at, and attachment to, a person you love. From having mixed emotions, we experience how emotions can be both complex and a block to feeling free.

Historical Note

Spinoza did not use the terms *psychoanalysis* or *unconscious*, yet there is a sense in his ethics that he was aware of how forces could act on people unconsciously, in a restrictive way in particular. This is an understanding that was taken up and developed in the early twentieth century and has proved a valuable insight for therapeutic care.

Power of External Causes Exceeds the Mind's Power

Spinoza emphasises that the power of our mind to overcome the restrictive effect of external causes is limited. It is an unequal contest between the power of all that can affect our behaviour and the power we have to relate to it through a detached insight into it as a causal process. All we can do is survey the process and relate our experiences to it, but we can't prevent the events occurring that lead to our own frustration at (in an earlier example) losing the care report. Nor can we prevent the causes of certain events occurring that greatly affect us, such as our ageing and dying. As he says, 'The force with which a man persists in existing is limited, and is far surpassed by the power of external causes' (144–5). External causes 'far surpass human power or virtue' (124).

In particular, how other people are affected by, and respond to, all that causes their behaviour is outside our control. A big source of the causes acting on us comes from how other people's behaviour impacts on us (84–5). Everyone is *liable to emotions* that particularly make us *inconstant and variable*. As a result, people are 'often drawn in different directions and are contrary one to the other, while they need each other's help' (165). If what Spinoza is saying is true, it will be difficult for anyone to have control over what affects them for their own benefit. Consequently, we can understand that it will be all the more difficult for social care clients, especially those who have deep-seated problems. It will be hard for them to have the kind of detachment required to be able to manage the emotional causes of their behaviour. This, in turn, serves to highlight an aspect of the role of the care worker in enabling clients to gain greater awareness of factors contributing to their need for care – as part of the process of helping them to develop their well-being.

If Spinoza is right about emotions causing our actions, then he is providing strong understanding why we should empathise with people in their difficulties and challenges. Even if he is only partially right, he is still revealing to us a powerful factor that acts on us to influence our actions.

Freedom as Awareness of Causes

At the same time, while Spinoza does not believe we have free will, he believes that the more *we are aware* of this as our condition, the more we can liberate our behaviour from being blindly dictated by causes. He expresses this by saying that when we become aware of factors that affect our choices, this has the effect of increasing *our active power* over that which is causing our behaviour. We are then, if you like, acting less blindly or in the dark, or, as he puts it, we are less *passively restricted*. Also, the more we manage to have this awareness as a clear and distinct idea in coping with the experiences life throws up, the more we are behaving ethically. It is, for him, the essence of being ethical. He understands good and bad in relation to whether we strive to have clear awareness of the causes acting on us, or whether we simply allow ourselves to be driven by them unaware (147). To be virtuous is to have power over whatever is affecting us from the point of view of regarding it as caused in us. This is because our mind can then be less restricted and more active (143).

Ethics as Living Power for Ourselves and Others

For Spinoza, the terms *good* and *bad* refer only to the means of achieving this greater active power of mind or living power for ourselves. It is the essence of ethics. 'We call that good or bad which is useful or the contrary to our preservation, that is, which increases or diminishes, helps or hinders our power of acting' (147). Here we find one of the ways of understanding the ethical roots of self-empowerment. Moreover, it is the kind of power that also directly benefits others. Once we are acting according to reason in this way and recognise the true nature of what is to the advantage of our living power, we will recognise that we desire the same for others (153). He gives three particular reasons for this.

Common Advantage

Like Aristotle, he points to the obvious fact that no one is self-sufficient. It stands to reason that we should unite with others for mutual benefit. 'From the common society of men far more conveniences arise than the contrary' (161).

Human Nature

He also points out that helping others is in our nature. We are naturally altruistic. 'For he who is moved neither by reason nor pity to help others is rightly called inhuman, for he seems to be so unlike a man' (173).

Improved Human Relations

If everybody is seeking his own genuine good by increasing his living power in accordance with having awareness of the causal process at work in his responses and actions, then each person will be pulling in the same direction. As a result, we will be less likely to act restrictively toward each other by, for example, venting our restrictive or negative emotions on others. Also, we will be more inclined to act to increase other people's living power because then they will be less inclined to act restrictively toward us. As he puts it, 'Only free men are truly useful to one another and are united by the closest bond of friendship and endeavour to benefit each other with an equal impulse of love' (185).

Empathy and Fortitude

Since we are subject to external causes that restrict our capacity to achieve the good through increased living power, we need to have empathy for each other and to work together for our mutual benefit. In this effort to be ethical, the virtue of fortitude has a prominent place. Fortitude normally has the meaning of having strength to withstand adversity and setback and to persist in trying to do what we believe is right. In relation to his ethics, Spinoza (124) divides fortitude into:

- Courage to persist in trying to have the one measure of freedom available to us, which is freedom of mind in being aware that our behaviour is determined by a causal process, and to do this especially by developing *presence of mind* when in danger of allowing emotional reaction to rule us restrictively.
- Generosity to help others by joining with them in trying to have mutual increased living power rather than be a hindrance.

The Causal Process as 'God or Nature'

Before leaving Spinoza's ethics, there is an aspect central to his theory that needs mention, and it is one that helps to deepen the understanding of the need for empathy. This point can be difficult to understand, but let's try. When Spinoza speaks of becoming aware of what is causing our behaviour, he is not referring so much to particular causes in any particular situation which we may be able to identify, such as our emotion of anger. Instead, he is referring to the whole, chain-like causal process itself that is operating in the universe, and he terms this 'God or Nature'. By 'God or Nature' he does not mean the God of traditional religions, a personal all-powerful being. Instead, he is referring to an impersonal causal force of all that occurs, our own behaviour included. It arrives in us in our behaviour at any given moment as an aspect of how it is working itself out. By reflecting on what is happening to us, he says we can have an 'intuitive knowledge' of God or Nature as the adequate cause (69). 'God or Nature' is the only adequate (or full) cause of what is going on in us (140). The reason why this awareness is so important is because, since this is the essence of what is going on, when we become aware of it, *we are enabling it to have an effect* on our mind, *an effect* of making our mind more active (or powerful) in line with it. Our awareness then feeds into the heart of the causal process, connecting directly with it as it is occurring through us. With this awareness, God or Nature is in us, he says, as the essence of our mind (84–5). Heady stuff!

CONCLUSION ON EMPATHY AS A SOCIAL CARE VALUE

In society, people are limited in what they can do by the extent to which their circumstances and capacities restrict their sphere of activities in ways for which they are not responsible. This, in itself, provides a reason for the value of having empathy for them as a basis for providing them with social care.

With regard to freedom of the will, ultimately it is impossible to know for certain the extent to which we have it, or even if we have it at all. How much free will is being exercised, for example, by family members torn apart by difficulties? Even though we have a strong subjective experience of having free will, it is not something that can be demonstrated to exist to the satisfaction of everybody. For practical purposes, notably for holding people responsible for their behaviour, both morally and under the law, free will is assumed to exist. If free will did not exist, it would make no sense to blame or praise people for their actions. Without free will there is no personal responsibility. There is also a danger, especially in care work, that we may show a lack of respect for the capacity people have if we relate to them on the basis that they do not have free will. At the same time, we accept that free will can be reduced by influences acting on people which incline them to behave in a particular way. The justice system allows for such influences as mitigating factors where they can be shown to have reduced a person's free exercise of his will in committing an offence.

Social care practices related to having empathy in caring for clients include:

- Providing encouragement and support for clients' efforts (as opposed to exhortation and expectancy).
- Accepting the client as an individual, for the person s/he has become in relation to his/her circumstances no matter what s/he may have done in the past.
- Recognising reasons for reduced responsibility.
- Being non-judgmental, i.e. avoiding narrow, moralistic judgments.

Empathy is also central for enabling care workers to build good interpersonal relations with clients, relations built especially on trust. Banks writes about the growing trend in the management of social work which emphasises the requirement for social work practitioners to record their accountability to written regulations and procedures in a variety of different types of cases. This, she argues, can lead in practice to a lessening of the importance of interpersonal relations between the professional and the client, and even to distrust. The understandable context of a greater emphasis on management and accountability places a challenge to the maintenance of the traditional, core, social-care value of empathy. (See Banks 2004: Chapters 6 and 7, and also Banks 2006: Chapter 6.)

CASE STUDY 7.1

Case Study: Empathy and Allowing for Exception

Consider the case of a family of asylum seekers whose children have been attending school in Ireland for over a year (or perhaps a shorter period) and who have become part of the local community. They now find that their application for asylum has been turned down because the details they gave in their application were found not to be in accordance with the facts. They have been issued with notice that they are to be deported back to the country of their origin, where welfare services are undeveloped and where they are likely to face serious poverty. Having regard to reasons for empathy, consider and discuss the response Irish society should have to the family's needs. Include in your study of the case Kant's principles, which include a duty to tell the truth (as well as the criticism of his principles that they can be harsh in not allowing for exceptions) together with his principles to respect and care for others.

Question for Consideration and Discussion

Are psychological and social pressures (e.g. criminality in family background, lack of educational opportunity, unemployment, peer pressure) adequate reasons to relieve people of responsibility for actions generally considered morally wrong?

Moral Challenge and Empathy for Characters in Novels and Films

Some novels and films can be of absorbing interest from the way the characters handle moral challenges. They are frequently the kind of challenges we can imagine ourselves having in different, if less dramatic, circumstances. This is particularly the case where the challenge is not presented in black and white, but in shades of grey. By this I mean that from the circumstances portrayed there can be understandable reasons why people act as they do, even though at some level they know it is wrong and likely to get them into trouble with other people and usually also with the law, or else they know their action is right and are determined to do right even though it will get them into trouble. Such novels and films also show how people can be led by their emotions, by desire or anger or care for others which proves to be their downfall, or their heroism. Check out *The House of Sand and Fog* and *The Constant Gardener*.

Exercise 7.1

Describe a moral challenge experienced by a character(s) in a novel or film that has struck you, and give an account of the way the character(s) handled the challenge in the light of your understanding of free will and determinism.

CRITICAL EVALUATION

Spinoza's View of Behaviour as Determined

One point of criticism is that Spinoza seems to assume that just because we can see that lots of things in the world are caused, e.g. that a foot striking a ball causes it to move, this does not have to mean that everything is caused, in particular human behaviour. Spinoza is said to have been influenced by the scientific view current in his time (in the seventeenth century) of a mechanised world in which everything has a cause. But, in having consciousness, human beings can be considered different in being able to act freely.

At the same time, he is recognised for having shown the powerful and volatile role emotions play in contributing to behaviour.

Kant and the Problem of Free Will

In his ethics, Kant came up against a particular difficulty in being able to show how we have free will. From a social care perspective, this difficulty can also help in understanding why people may not be in charge of their lives and so be deserving of empathy.

For Kant, as we saw, the *will* is central. It is only those principles that we can *will* to become universal laws which establish how we should behave. But, for Kant, it is crucial that we regard the will as free in its *willing* of principles as universal laws (Kant 1969: 109). This is because if our *will* is influenced by forces external to it, then it is those forces that cause us to will the universal laws and not the *will* itself. This is why, for him, the will has to be seen as *autonomous*, i.e. something free in itself and not determined by outside influences. Such outside influences typically include any of the things that give rise to our inclinations or desires. On the face of it, some inclination or desire affects how we behave, and Kant accepts this. He goes further and claims that our behaviour is always *caused* by some inclination or desire. This means he is faced with a contradiction. On the one hand, he is saying our behaviour is always caused, and on the other hand he is saying we have to regard our *will* as free in how it *wills* moral principles. So the question is, how can the apparent contradiction be resolved? How can our will be free while at the same time our actions are always caused or determined for us?

Free Will as a Presupposition

Kant's answer is detailed and can be difficult to understand. At the outset he accepts that 'the idea of freedom' of the will is merely 'a presupposition' (109). He accepts that he has not proved it exists, and he does not think the existence of free will can be proved. To find a proof for it would mean having to go beyond the bounds of knowledge. However, he does try to explain how the freedom of the will can be understood in relation to *willing* principles as universal laws.

The Two Standpoints

By way of explaining how we have free will, he says we can look on ourselves from 'two standpoints'. From one standpoint our actions are caused – from the other we have free will. From one standpoint we live in the world of sense experience, of sight, hearing, etc. This is the world as we experience it through our five senses. He calls it 'the sensible world'. This world is the world as it appears to us, the world of appearances. It is the world as we can only know it in its relation to us. In belonging to this world, our behaviour is caused by our inclinations and desires.

In the sensible world, considered on its own, we do not have free will. If we ask ourselves why we have behaved in such a way, some inclination or desire will appear to our 'inner sense' as the reason. So, for example, if I go for a walk, it is because it appears to my inner sense I did so because I wanted to take exercise. (Kant was so well known for always taking a daily walk at the same time each day that the story goes that the townspeople used to know what time it was by seeing him leave his house!) We are always able to find some reason why we behave, and so in this world of the senses we are not free. Our behaviour is always *caused* by something or other; it is not the outcome of free will or free choice.

This is the first standpoint from which we can look on ourselves, the standpoint of living in a sensible world where our actions are governed by our inclinations and desires.

But, for Kant, we can also look on ourselves from a second standpoint. This standpoint is one in which we must assume another world existing behind all appearances of things in the sensible world. This is a world of things, not in their relation to us but simply in relation to themselves, a world of 'things in themselves'. We cannot know this world as it is in itself, but only in the way in which it affects us through appearances. We must assume that this 'intelligible world' exists if we are to make sense of our experience of having freedom of the will (111–112).

How does this solve the apparent contradiction of finding that our behaviour is both free and caused at the same time? Kant explains this by simply saying we belong to both worlds. When we act to *will* a principle as a universal law, we are solely in the intellectual world where there is freedom. But when we want to know what we should do in some situation that arises, we belong both to the sensible world, the world governed by desire and inclination, *and* to the intellectual world. This means we can respond with free will and either go with, or go against, a particular desire by acting in accordance with principles we can *will* as universal laws. Through having a foot in both worlds at the same time, we are placed precisely in the experience of moral concern or challenge in that we can either do as we ought and act in conformity to universal law or we can allow ourselves to be governed by a desire or inclination that is contrary to it (113).

Difficulties with Kant's Account of Free Will

Kant's account of the problem of free will is generally acknowledged to be both difficult and obscure, and critics have found fault with it. One problem Kant leaves us with is that we have no idea how our deliberations in the intelligible world can act upon the sensible world (Benn 1998: 100). There is no obvious bridge between them, since Kant sees them as quite separate.

From a social care point of view, the difficulties Kant encounters in trying to explain free will show just how difficult it is for people to know for certain that they have free will and are responsible for their actions. Even if Kant is right, it is still a major challenge for people to use their free will in practice and to appropriately address the pressures they feel acting upon them as causes of their actions.

As he says, in our ordinary everyday experience our actions are not merely influenced by our inclinations and desires, but actually caused by them. Thus it is a task for the intellectual side of our nature, where our freedom resides, to combat these causes where the need arises, assuming it is possible, through exercising free will.

Especially from a social care point of view, Kant's difficulty with the problem helps bring out how people are likely to have difficulty relating clearly to free will in themselves as a means to avoid behaving in ways that are not good for them, or to behave in a different way to improve their independence.

REVIEW

The problems associated with freedom, in its challenge and in its restrictions, and in understanding free will provide ground for the value of having empathy for people in the difficulties they face in their lives. This, in turn, can be seen to underlie the justification of providing them with services to remove or alleviate those difficulties.

FURTHER READING

Benn, P. (1998) *Ethics*, UCL Press (Chapter 6).

REFERENCES

Banks, S. (2004) *Ethics, Accountability and the Social Professions*, Palgrave Macmillan.
Kant, I. (1969) *The Moral Law: Kant's Groundwork of the Metaphysic of Morals*, translated and analysed by H. Patton, Hutcheson University Library, London.
Sartre, J. (1995) *Being and Nothingness*, Routledge.
Spinoza, B. de (1995) *Ethics*, Everyman.

8
Acceptance of Difference

OVERALL AIM

To explain why individuals and cultures can have different moral beliefs with a view to understanding the value of acceptance of difference, especially in the context of a multicultural society.

LEARNING OUTCOMES

At the end of this chapter you should be able to:

- Explain why morals can be considered relative to a person or culture (relativism).
- Explain how moral relativism follows from Moore's view that it is a mistake to identify good with anything that occurs naturally, such as a desire for well-being.
- Explain the arguments for relativism from egoism and cultural difference.
- Relate a relativist view to the value of accepting moral difference.
- Explain the criticisms that can be made of the relativist position.
- Recognise that there are limits to practices that can be considered acceptable.
- Recognise that under relativism, the basis for providing social care is a matter of personal or cultural belief rather than an independent moral requirement.

INTRODUCTION

For people who work in social care, an important value is to have the same regard for all people, regardless of how different their values are from the ones they hold themselves or from the main public values operative in society. Acceptance of difference in relation to the Travelling community has been an issue in Irish society. Acceptance of difference is a value of particular importance now in Ireland as the country is becoming increasingly made up of diverse cultural groups due to immigration. We are now a society in which there are a number of minority cultural groups whose values are based on ethnicity or religion, or both. Apart from people from Eastern European countries, there are now communities from African countries such as Nigeria, Middle Eastern countries and China. Acceptance of difference helps provide for a society in which all people are treated equally and in which members of all cultural groups are integrated into the society and feel they belong. It is a value that shows respect for people's independence and right to live in accordance with values they see as appropriate. In providing care services for families from different cultural backgrounds, care workers will come across examples of practices that reflect different value systems to those of Irish society, for example, in relation to the authority and role of fathers and mothers and in relation to different expectancies for male and female children. Gender equality, which is an important value in Irish society, may or may not be reflected to the same extent in the relations some cultures value between men and women.

First we will look at some reasons why we should accept other people's values even though we may disagree with them. One source of justification for moral difference is moral relativism. Moral relativism is the view that there is no common set of values which can be shown to apply for everyone. Instead, values are relative to an individual or culture, and this provides justification for why values can vary. Moral relativism is not the only source that supports the value of acceptance of difference. As part of human rights, for example, people have cultural rights. They have the right to manifest their religion or belief alone, or in community with others, in public or private. This is acknowledged in both Article 18 of the UN Declaration and Article 9 of the European Convention on Human Rights.

RELATIVISM

Objective and Subjective Truth

Moral relativism is the view that a common ethical basis for everyone cannot be established. Instead, our morals are always related to something from which they come, such as our feelings, ego, our culture or society. In this way, morals are said to vary between individuals and between social groups. In general, moral relativism is the view that morals are not *objectively* true. That is, they cannot be shown to be true by any independent evidence that is compelling for everybody. Instead, morals are merely *subjectively* true, i.e. true only for the person who holds them in relation to their own thoughts, feelings, time in history or cultural upbringing.

Moral Authority

One way of understanding relativism is to see that there isn't a single moral authority which everyone accepts as binding on them. For many, the authority lies in the teachings of their particular religious belief, while for others it is the norms of their society, and for others again it is their own individual viewpoint or their conscience.

Origin of Relativism

The view that morals can be considered relative has been recognised for a long time, but it wasn't until the twentieth century that it has become a common ethical position. The ancient Greek philosopher, Protagoras (480–411 BC), expressed a relativist position when he said, 'A human being is the measure of all things . . .' (Woodruff 1999: 292). Applied to morals, this means that it is up to each person to decide for himself/herself what has value and what does not. Wong (2004: 433) speculates that Protagoras is likely to have been led to his relativist view from contact between his own culture and others from which he learned that different cultures have different moral beliefs.

Modern Relativism

Interpretation is a word we can perhaps now identify with quite readily. Often when we disagree with someone over whether a particular practice is morally right or wrong we may say, 'Well that's your interpretation, but it's not mine.' In doing so, we are recognising the subjective nature of viewpoints. In the nineteenth century, Nietzsche claimed that no actions are good or bad in themselves – it is only our interpretation of them that makes them good or bad: 'There is no such thing as moral phenomena, but only moral interpretations of phenomena' (1989: 91).

The publication in 1903 of G. Moore's book, *Principia Ethica*, did much to make a relativist position common. This was not because he himself put forward a specifically relativist position, but because he pointed out that there was no way anybody could ever really know what good and bad are. If good cannot be known, this leaves it open to people to associate good with nothing at all or with whatever they want. Moore's ethics is famous for an insight known as 'the Naturalistic Fallacy' (1962: 10). He pointed out that it is a fallacy (an error) to think that good can be defined as something in particular which is a natural feature of human experience, such as the desire for well-being. In the next section we will look at the fallacy as a means of understanding why it leaves the question of good and bad open to being understood in different ways.

Relativism is quite a common position for people to hold today. It is associated in particular with individualism. This is the idea that each individual is his/her own moral authority and there is no authority which can bind us to common moral standards.

MOORE'S INSIGHT: THE NATURALISTIC FALLACY

For Moore, disagreement between philosophers about ethics is based on confusion. This is because philosophers have always assumed that the subject of ethics – the good – can be defined. But this is a false assumption. If something is able to be defined, then it can be broken down into parts in which the essential part unique to it is identified in the context of its other parts, which it may share with other things. For example, a pen can be defined by a nib or ballpoint that enables a person to write, while at the same time it shares having ink and tubing with other objects. In this sense *pen* is a complex object and can be broken down into its parts to define exactly what it is. But *good* is not like this at all. It cannot be broken down into anything else (1962: 7–8). Good is simply good. 'If I am asked, "What is good?" my answer is that good is good, and that is the end of the matter' (6). Actually, for Moore it's not quite 'the end of the matter' since he had a lot more to say about it! Moore calls good 'a simple notion' just like yellow or any other colour (7). You simply know what it means. It cannot be defined or explained. He says we have an intuition of good, but all he means by having an intuition is that we do not know what good is.

Moore emphasises that we have no intuition of some mental content or mysterious substance which could be substituted for the good. As he puts it, 'there is nothing whatsoever which we could substitute for good, and that is what I mean when I say it is indefinable'(8).

Relativism Arising from Moore's Insight

If Moore is right, then, in practice, it makes morals relative to whatever a person sees good to be. Since good is not anything that can be defined, and since our only knowledge of good consists of this recognition through a blank intuition, it is, if you like, up to each person to fill in the blank intuition of what good means for themselves. This, then, will make morals relative to people's intuitions.

Moore, as I said, did not put forward a specifically relativist position, but it is a consequence of his view. He believed that in practice we could, and did, have intuitions of certain things as good. He also suggests we all have the same intuition of what things are good in practice. He called them 'practical goods'. I will mention them briefly in the next section. But bear in mind that because Moore's intuition of what good is in practical terms is *only his intuition*, however much his intuition may appear to make sense, other people could validly have a different intuition of what good is.

Moore's Intuition of Practical Goods

The main thing our intuition of practical goods relates to is 'the pleasures of human intercourse' or 'personal affection' (188). He claims this is something we can all recognise. In practice, this means having a civilised society (158). So, a rule against murder is an obvious example of a rule we need. Other rules that help make life pleasurable for everyone include 'industry, temperance and the keeping of promises' (157).

Relativism Still the Likely Outcome

However, Moore still sticks to his view that we have no means of knowing, either by reasoning or feeling or willing, that these practical goods which he mentions are good (141). We are faced with having to accept that things we recognise as good are so from self-evidence. The result is that, while Moore's list of things that are good may appeal to us, we don't have to accept them. We could still validly give priority to fulfilling our plans and activities as the main good for us without regard to the effect doing so may have on others. It is because of this that his view provides understanding for a relativist view of morals.

If relativists are right and people can have their own morality, this provides a reason for the value of accepting people's moral beliefs where they differ from our own. We cannot prove our values are superior, nor can they for their values – so acceptance of difference is justified.

TWO SPECIFIC ARGUMENTS FOR RELATIVISM

These are:

- Psychological egoism.
- Cultural difference.

Psychological Egoism

This is the argument that all of our acts are done to satisfy our ego, that they have self-interest or self-regard as their primary motive. Egoists point to the prevalence in society of people acting primarily to satisfy their own interests and desires, such as for wealth, power or pleasure. In our interpersonal relations, egoists say we are always suiting ourselves in one way or another.

Psychological egoists in particular argue that even if we think we are acting for the sake of some ideal or principle, such as concern for others, we are either deluding ourselves or being hypocritical. They are not saying we always act in an obviously selfish way. However, they are saying that in every act there is a self-regarding element, and that this is the element for which we do the act. They claim they can always identify a self-regarding motive. For example, they will point out one of the following reasons why we are kind to others:

- To increase our chances of receiving kindness in return.
- To feel good about ourselves.

- To avoid feeling bad or guilty.
- To ensure others think well of us or to earn praise.
- To feel satisfied from living up to our beliefs.

If we protest that none of those self-regarding reasons explains why we want to act kindly, they will simply say that it must be for some other self-regarding reason.

If egoists are right, then there is invariably a self-regarding reason behind our behaviour. We may find this unappealing, but for egoists it is the reality and, as such, we should accept it for what it is. How, then, does psychological egoism lead to the value of acceptance of difference? Well, if the theory is right and we always act out of self-interest, it means we have understanding for why people may justifiably differ in the values they hold because they see it to be in their self-interest to hold those values.

Cultural Difference

This relativist argument claims that ethical requirements are *nothing more than* those that happen to be part of our particular culture. Ethics, in other words, can be reduced to the views that members of a culture have about certain practices. Morality is no more than the conduct that happens to be approved of, or disapproved of, in one culture or another.

In secular liberal cultures, for example, gender equality is an important moral value, understood as men and women having equal rights. However, some Islamic cultures value a different relation between men and women. Muslim communities vary in the practices they consider acceptable for expressing the relationship and some are more liberal than others. But, in its stricter forms as practiced in Saudi Arabia, for example, women are not allowed to vote or to drive. Also, it is common for families to arrange the marriage of their daughters. Women also have to dress modestly in a loose robe (abaya) and head cover (hijab); a face veil (niqab) is optional.

Also, within Western culture, there are different Western subcultural groups who hold different moral beliefs. For example, within gay and lesbian culture, sex (and option of marriage) with a partner of the same sex is a morally important value. By contrast, within the Catholic cultural tradition, it is morally wrong. Also, for many within liberal culture the right to choose is an important value for such practices as abortion or euthanasia. By contrast, both practices are regarded as morally wrong by many others, in particular by members of religious cultures. Cultural difference also includes the acceptability of the death penalty for murder in many non-Western countries and some US states, whereas it is viewed as unacceptable in EU countries where it is banned.

Parekh makes the point that it is 'an obvious fact' that our culture shapes us in 'countless ways'. Our culture holds out to us particular ways of life and attachments as well as developing in us particular 'moral and psychological dispositions'

(2000: 11; 110). From our culture we learn what practices are acceptable and unacceptable, as well as how people can differ in their moral attitudes (156). Cultures express human capacity in different ways. Parekh cites the example of how Buddhist and Hindu cultures respect and care for the natural environment and for all forms of life, which for them are important moral values. In contrast, in Western cultures people generally consider their relations to the natural world to be outside the sphere of moral concern (144; 215). (In the West this view has been changing as a result of growing recognition that we are engaging in practices that cause environmental damage which adversely affects our well-being.)

As a result of cultures expressing human capacities in different ways, Parekh takes the view that no one culture's value system can be privileged over another's. In particular, he argues that Western societies should allow for the participation of the values and practices of minority cultural groups whose values relate to their particular culture, and not require them to be confined to the private sphere. Parekh argues the case for a fully multicultural society (a 'multiculturalist' society) where the values of minority cultures are included along with Western liberal values as part of society's operative public values.

Relativist Argument from Moral Change

To add to their argument that values are relative, relativists point to the fact that many moral beliefs within cultures change over time. They argue that if a practice was acceptable at one period in time and then becomes unacceptable, or was once considered unacceptable and then becomes acceptable, then this also shows that morals are the kind of things that vary and differ.

Many examples can be given to illustrate how moral views of certain practices have changed over time. For example, many white people in the southern states of the US up until the 1960s, and in South Africa until the 1990s, considered apartheid morally acceptable. In Ireland, up to the early 1970s it was considered morally (and legally) acceptable to pay women less than men for equal work. In the public service, women had to give up their jobs on marriage. Into the second half of the twentieth century, under Catholic moral practice it had been considered acceptable (by some) to punish young girls and women who were perceived to be engaged in prostitution, or who gave birth outside marriage, by effectively confining them to hard work in institutions known as *Magdalene Laundries*. They were also required to give their babies up for adoption. Also, for many people in Ireland moral attitudes toward sexual activity have changed significantly over the last fifty years in relation to sex outside marriage, single parenthood, contraception and gay and lesbian relationships.

It is because of such variations in moral beliefs between cultures, and because of variation over time, that relativists argue there is no set of moral requirements that can stand up as common for everyone.

Cultural Difference and Limits to Acceptance

While it is now a generally accepted value that it is a good thing to have acceptance for the values of other cultures as well as to develop appreciation for them as part of the recognition and celebration of cultural diversity, it is difficult to accept that all practices that have value for people within a culture are morally valid. Tolerance, in practice, does not require a person to be tolerant of everything. Andre Compte-Sponville makes this point strongly in a chapter on the virtue of tolerance (2002: 157–83).

A problem with accepting cultural relativism *fully* as grounds for acceptance of difference is that it would mean having to accept practices which we find unacceptable. A strong example is the practice of female circumcision or genital mutilation, which is still an accepted ritual practice, particularly in some African cultures. From the perspective of other cultures, and human rights especially, it is considered to be a violation of an individual female's bodily integrity which inflicts irreparable harm. It can take different forms. One form is the removal of the clitoris. The aim is to contain women's sexuality, in particular to preserve virginity until marriage. It is inflicted on babies as young as a few weeks, but usually on girls between four and fifteen. It has severe physical, psychological and sexual health consequences and can result in death. An *Irish Times* article by Kitty Holland (27 September 2004) reported a demand for the practice from some members of immigrant communities. It is illegal under the Offences against the Person Act, and there have been calls to make it illegal explicitly, especially as there are concerns that it may be occurring illegally.

People outside the particular cultures in which it is practised, and who do not accept it, are adamant that they are right, i.e. no girl or woman anywhere should ever be subjected to such treatment. In other words, such examples encourage the idea that there have to be some moral absolutes, i.e. practices considered wrong or right in themselves regardless of what is acceptable in certain cultures. Another way of putting this is to say that we pack a lot of emotional conviction into our disapproval of certain practices, and that the source for this disapproval must come from somewhere other than what is, or is not, culturally acceptable.

While Parekh takes the view that values are culturally embedded, he does not accept the full relativist position that values consist only of particular cultural beliefs. For example, he does not accept female circumcision or genital mutilation or gender inequality (2000: 277–284). He believes values come from interplay between culture and human nature to provide for different forms of the good life. Two of the basic features of human nature are that we each have 'a distinct self-consciousness with an inescapable inner life' and a need and desire for well-being (132–3). We have, then, to be able to show rationally that particular cultural practices, if they are to be acceptable, serve as valid expression of support for these features of human nature as opposed to damaging or suppressing them.

ACCEPTANCE AND SOCIAL CARE

Relativism provides understanding why people have different values. In doing so, it provides understanding of why the value of acceptance of moral difference is justified within limits. In particular, it helps us to understand why narrow moralistic judgment of other people's behaviour is not justified or acceptable in social care.

It also helps provide understanding for cultural integration, which is now important in Ireland given the growth in diversity and numbers of people from different ethnic and religious backgrounds living here. It helps to show that there is no moral basis for such practices as hate speech, racism and groups becoming ghettoised. It also helps to show there are no moral grounds for treating people unequally just because they have different values to the prevailing ones in society. Acceptance is not always an easy value to practise, in particular for those who hold strongly to their own moral beliefs as being the true ones. Compte-Sponville makes the point that there is an inevitable tension between 'truth' and tolerance. People who believe that their political, religious or secular liberal beliefs are *the truth* can find it difficult to have tolerance for practices incompatible with their truth. This is because, strictly speaking, the only value consistent with truth is acceptance of the truth and all that goes with it. This can set people against views other than their own. There is always a danger that conviction about being in possession of *the truth* can lead to intolerance and even fanaticism (2002: 163–5).

A second point about relativism, which has a social care implication, is that it supports the view that there is no compelling reason for people to have a moral obligation to care for others unless it is their personal choice or the belief of their culture which they accept. One version of relativism that has grown to have a lot of influence on society is individualism. Individualism supports the entitlement of each person to fulfil his/her own needs without any particular obligation to help others unless it is their choice. We will consider this viewpoint more closely in Chapter 9.

So far, I have been making the case for the relativity of values and for the way in which this can be taken to underlie the value of acceptance of moral difference within limits. In simple terms, who is to say who is right when it comes to morals? However, the relativist position is open to what can be considered valid criticisms, and we touched on one of them in dealing with the difficulty in accepting a fully relativist position which would mean having to accept practices we consider seriously wrong. We will look at these criticisms in the critical evaluation section.

Exercise 8.1

Think of your own examples of how morals have differed over time and how they differ between cultures. Consider what that tells you about ethics.

> # Question for Consideration and Discussion: Equality and Diversity
>
> At the start of 2005, France brought in a law banning the wearing of prominent religious symbols, including the Muslim headscarf (hijab), in public schools and public service employment. The government was concerned to maintain the secular nature of French society. They were also concerned that the wearing of the symbols was emphasising difference to an extent that took away from the core value of equality. In 2006, Britain debated limiting the wearing of face veils for being a barrier to intercultural communication. Consider where you stand on the issue.

CRITICAL EVALUATION

Moore's Detached View

Moore's view of good can be considered too detached. The practical reality is that people live through close engagement with what they see to be good and bad. We may not be able to define what good is in Moore's sense, but at the same time, we experience it as if we do know what it means in its connection to things we value.

Psychological Egoism: Difference between Personal Desire and Self-regard

The argument for psychological egoism can be faulted. Bond (2001: 7–20) argues that it rests on a confusion. He points out that yes, there is a strong personal element to why we act because all our acts are done to satisfy some desire that we have. But this does not have to mean that all our acts are done for a self-regarding motive. An act done for a personal desire can be a personal desire for the good of others, or it can be done primarily for the sake of others. This is different from doing it for a self-regarding motive. Of course, we can be kind to others for a self-regarding motive, but we can still act out of a desire for the good of others regardless of the amount of satisfaction it brings us. Bond says egoists have confused the statement 'all acts are self-regarding' with the statement 'all acts are done out of personal desire'. The first is false while the second is true.

Baier finds fault with egoism in a similar way to Bond. He says that even if we do have an egoistic motive for our actions, that 'does not make it the operative one' (Baier 2004: 199). In other words, our effective motive can be our desire for the well-being of others even if, mixed in with it, we also have the motive of satisfying our own needs in some way.

Cultural Difference: Distinction between Morals Being Part of Culture and Consisting of Culture

Some argue that because we are inevitably cultural in our viewpoint, we can never be in a position to make culturally neutral value judgments about cultural practices, and that we therefore have to respect people's practices no matter what those practices are. They argue that no one can transcend his/her own cultural background to make judgments from on *high*, as it were. In his essay 'Multiculturalism' Arthur gives Fish's view as follows: 'we cannot make "objective" judgments about cultures, but rather only ones from our own cultural vantage point' (2004: 430). However, this is not necessarily the case.

It is true that moral views about the same practices differ between cultures and also that within cultures they have changed radically over time, particularly in Western cultures. But does this mean that morality is *only* about what is culturally acceptable and unacceptable? There is a difference between saying that morality *arises for* people within their culture and saying that morality only *consists of* particular cultural attitudes. (See Bond 1996: 21–43 for more on this point.) If we accept that morality consists only of cultural attitudes and practices, then we would be obliged to accept those attitudes and practices because that would be all that morality meant. It would mean we should be able to have no problem accepting and following the practices of other cultures when we visited them. We would have to accept the old advice that 'when in Rome, do as the Romans do'. If we lived in ancient times and visited Rome, we would have to accept their practice of feeding Christians and criminals to the lions. But the reality is that we don't morally accept the practices of other cultures where those practices conflict with our moral view.

In addition, changes in moral attitudes considered for the better in any culture only come about because people feel that current attitudes are unacceptable and voice criticism. This, too, indicates that people have a sense of morality that does not always coincide with that of their time in history or culture. If morality consisted solely of what happened to be acceptable in our culture, why would anyone be activated to bring about change? So, against the relativist argument that moral change over time justifies the view that morals are relative to a culture at a certain time, we can argue that the demand for change indicates a source for morality that is not reducible to a culture's beliefs at any particular time. We could argue that over time we are becoming clearer about what is morally acceptable and what is not, and the reason for this transcends people's personal views or their cultural practices, whether this reason lies in cross-cultural influence and dialogue, which Parekh believes, or in human rights or some other source. Moral change suggests that in some way we ultimately get our sense of ethics from somewhere else besides culture and our time.

The Relativist Position in Practice

In practice, few, if any, relativists will go so far as to accept or advocate the full implication of their ethical position, which is that a free-for-all in morality is justified. They tend to accept a version of Hobbes's social contract view of ethics, which we will look at in Chapter 10. This is the view that as a matter of social convenience, we should all agree that certain behaviour is right or wrong. It is a view of ethics based on what is called *collective* or *enlightened* self-interest. It supports the value of providing at least some care for those in need so that society will be better for everyone through having fewer social problems.

At the same time, relativism can – and does – contribute to a climate of scepticism about the existence of *higher* standards which have to be followed. This can result in not according much, if any, weight to moral arguments that go beyond self-interest for why an action should or should not be taken. This is notably the case in international relations where one theory known as *realist* stresses that a country's self-interest is the best basis for dealing with other countries.

Relativist Position as Self-contradictory

Finally, there is an old philosophical argument that some find convincing as a means of disproving the relativist position. The argument goes like this: relativists say no one is in a position to judge that the morals of a person or culture are better than any other because morals are always relative. In other words, there is no general truth applying for everybody where morals are concerned.

However, this statement *itself* amounts to at least *one* general truth, i.e. the truth that morals are always relative. So, if the relativist's statement of its own position can be true in universal application, there is no reason why other claims about morality could not also apply universally.

Put another way, by insisting that there are only various partial truths, relativists are insisting on this as a general truth. Thus they are contradicting themselves. In any event, if we can only have relative or partial truth from the perspective of our own culture, how can we be so sure that there are no general truths applying to all cultures? There still could well be general truths; the possibility is not ruled out, even if we can't prove it.

REVIEW

Relativism is the view that there is no common morality. Instead, morals are relative to a person or culture. This view provides understanding for differences in moral beliefs among people in society, especially a society shared by people of different cultural traditions. A relativist understanding is one way by which the value of acceptance of other people's values and practices can be supported. It also supports an integrated society in which people of all cultural backgrounds are treated equally and have equal opportunities. Criticisms of relativism also show that it is limited in providing a complete account of people's moral experience.

FURTHER READING

Benn, P. (1998) *Ethics*, UCL Press (Chapter 2).

Compte-Sponville, A. (2002) *A Short Treatise on the Great Virtues: The Uses of Philosophy in Everyday Life*, Heinemann (Chapter 13 on 'Tolerance').

REFERENCES

Baier, K. (2004) 'Egoism' in *A Companion to Ethics*, P. Singer (ed.) Blackwell.

Bond, E. (2001) *Ethics and Human Well-Being: An Introduction to Moral Philosophy*, Blackwell.

Compte-Sponville, A. (2002) *A Short Treatise on the Great Virtues: The Uses of Philosophy in Everyday Life*, Heinemann.

Fish (2003) cited in 'Multiculturalism' by John Arthur in *The Oxford Handbook of Practical Ethics*, H. LaFollette (ed.), Oxford University Press.

Moore, G. (1962) *Principia Ethica*, Cambridge University Press.

Nietzsche, F. (1989) *Beyond Good and Evil*, Prometheus Books.

Parekh, B. (2000) *Rethinking Multiculturalism: Cultural Diversity and Political Theory*, Palgrave Macmillan.

Wong, D. (2004) 'Relativism' in *A Companion to Ethics*, P. Singer (ed.), Blackwell.

Woodruff, P. (1999) 'Rhetoric and Relativism: Protagoras and Gorgias' in *The Cambridge Companion to Early Greek Philosophy*, A. Long (ed.), Cambridge University Press.

9

Social Well-being

OVERALL AIM

To show that society needs people to practise virtues if it is to function well.

LEARNING OUTCOMES

At the end of this chapter you should be able to:

- Explain the crisis MacIntyre claims exists in ethics because of individualism ('emotivism').
- Explain the effect of emotivism on the way people relate to each other and on the growth of social problems.
- Explain why people need to practise virtues to have a society in which there is social well-being.
- Define virtues as the means needed to obtain the goods internal to social practices.
- Understand the social practice of having concern and care for others as central to social well-being and explain why virtues such as compassion, courage and justice are needed to enable society to benefit from the goods internal to it.

INTRODUCTION

One of the consequences of relativism is that it has given rise to a view that when it comes to what people should, or should not, do, they can suit themselves. However, if people behave on this basis, then it will have negative effects on social well-being. For social well-being, society needs people to practise virtues such as restraining their own needs and desires in the interests of others. In caring for clients, care workers can come up against the lack of practice of virtues due to self-interested behaviour. For example, a range of social problems from family breakdown to serious crime can be considered to owe their existence in some part at least to self-interested behaviour. Parents may pursue their own desires to an extent that they neglect their children, resulting in the family needing support. A young person may satisfy his immediate desires by discharging his frustration in anti-social behaviour, or in offences such as joy riding, vandalism or theft. In each case, the problems their behaviour caused could be avoided by the practice of virtues of restraint and regard for the interests of others. This is not to say that lack of the practice of virtues is the simple cause of social problems. Factors such as poverty, lack of parenting skill and negative peer pressure make the lack of practice of virtues understandable and their practise difficult. The consumerist climate of society can also make it difficult for people to practise the virtues. Consuming is one of the main prevailing patterns of social behaviour. Also, material success is increasingly vaunted and celebrated above other values. However, some people don't have the means to obtain goods which others take for granted. Also, 'white collar crime', in the bad example it sets, can make it difficult for them to see why they should try to remain virtuous.

Care workers come up against lack of resources to meet care needs, especially resources such as staff or increased services. If there was more practice of the virtues of compassion and justice in political decisions on behalf of society as a whole, this would lead to more resources being made available. However, this is unlikely to happen to the extent needed unless people in general practise virtues, and also want and expect politicians to provide for care as a priority rather than add to the standard of living of those who are already quite well-off.

As we saw in Chapter 3, Aristotle brings out the interrelation between personal and social well-being. In his 1981 book, *After Virtue*, MacIntyre restated and developed Aristotle's view in the light of the growing trend he saw for people in modern Western societies to ignore the need to practise virtues in order to provide for social well-being.

There are many social practices that are good for people, such as family life, business and sport. MacIntyre points out that we need to practise the virtues if we are to obtain the goods internal to such social practices. A particular social practice that provides for the well-being of society is concern and care for others. It also requires people to practise virtues such as compassion and justice, and have the courage to speak out and act against indifference and opposition (MacIntyre 1985: 91–2). A good incentive to care and have concern is a society in which there are fewer social problems. Another good it gives rise to is a strong sense of community as opposed to division. Thus for MacIntyre, virtues have the status of being much more than good qualities which people may or may not have – they are social needs on which society depends if it is to function well.

VIRTUE IN OLDER SOCIETIES

In older *heroic* societies, such as in ancient Greece, Ireland and Iceland, MacIntyre contends that people had clear recognition of the vital role that virtues played in protecting the society and keeping it together. These virtues included courage, loyalty and providing practical assistance. This recognition is something which has been lost in modern society (122–3; 127).

THE CRISIS IN ETHICS

MacIntyre points out that up to the period between the seventeenth and eighteenth centuries in the Western world, the period known as the *Enlightenment*, ethics dealt with good and bad in relation to what people believed to be the purpose of human life. In practice, what people considered good was bound up with maintaining social bonds to the family and community. It was also bound up with religious belief. Ethics related to living out the purpose of human life in social and religious terms. However, from the Enlightenment period to modernity there was a move away from understanding ethics in terms of a person's social and religious involvement to seeing it in terms of an individual's own preference.

ORIGINS OF ETHICAL INDIVIDUALISM

The following developments are said to have contributed to individualism.

Science and Technology

All the practical benefits which have come from science and technology have served to emphasise how much we are at the centre of a world we have created for ourselves. It has served to emphasise what we can do for ourselves.

The Market Economy

This has enabled most of us to earn money surplus to meeting our basic needs. As a result, we have been able to do more to provide ourselves with the particular kind of life we want.

Politics Based on Individual Rights and Freedom

The democratic political system has meant that society came to be seen as serving the individual's needs rather than the individual serving the needs of society.

GROWTH OF INDIVIDUALISM

These developments have brought about major advances in human well-being in the modern period. However, they all contribute to positioning the individual at the centre of his/her life and, for MacIntyre, there is a downside to this in that it has led to a loosening of ties between individual and community well-being. Increasingly in ethics, people began to see that it was up to them to decide on their own morals. It has given rise to the view that morals are a matter for ourselves and that there is no common authority we have to accept. Morals became relative to a person's own views rather than related to some accepted common authority. This, in turn, has adversely affected the well-being of society as a whole.

In particular, many people felt restricted in how they wanted to live by a moral authority that bound them to social obligations and religious belief. People felt oppressed by demands made on them for the good of the community or the good of their soul. These demands were seen as preventing the individual from pursuing his/her own fulfilment.

Placing emphasis on the individual as a moral authority resulted in greater liberation from external authority. But the price paid was the loss of *any* generally accepted authority. This, MacIntyre claims, has resulted in a crisis in ethics whereby the well-being of society has suffered.

THE EMOTIVIST ATTITUDE

MacIntyre calls this movement to an ethics based on individual authority *emotivism*. Emotivism is the view that ethical values and principles are expressions of personal attitudes, preferences and choices (33–4). The common phrase 'look after number one' expresses the emotivist attitude. It is the attitude whereby a person feels entitled to indulge himself/herself as s/he pleases without social obligation. For example, an emotivist attitude allows people to feel free to change their mind if they want to and break a promise. Another example is the attitude summed up in the phrase 'greed is good', a view expressed in an address to his company's stockholders by Gordon Gekko, a wealthy and ruthless business character in the 1987 film *Wall Street*.

MacIntyre describes three general types of behaviour common in Western societies that characterise the emotivist view (24–31). They indicate patterns of behaviour that have replaced an acceptance of shared values. He believes many people now in Western societies have come to behave in accordance with these patterns to a greater or lesser extent.

Three Types of Emotivist Attitude

The Bureaucratic Manager

He matches means to ends in order to achieve efficiency without taking into account the personal effect his decisions will have on others. For example, he makes his workers redundant and relocates his factory in a country where wage costs are lower. The manager claims he is morally neutral in his work. He is merely trying to use means (money, materials and people) efficiently to achieve a goal of making a profit. But this type of behaviour is not morally neutral. It puts profit before people. It involves, in effect, manipulating people without feeling any moral requirement to contribute to their well-being.

Sometimes the ethical implications of decisions are ignored for economic reasons. Other times they are considered, but set aside in favour of economic gain. A clash between ethical and economic considerations occurs regularly. Remember the film *Jaws*. Sheriff Brody wanted to close the beach after the first shark attack, but the mayor wanted to keep the beach open because of its attraction for holidaymakers whose spending in the local town was important for its citizens. Economics took precedence over ethics: the beach stayed open and more people were attacked by the shark. While there can also be ethics on the economics side, such as protecting the good of people's livelihoods, decisions dictated by economic interests can be detrimental to the well-being of others, and this is not taken into account sufficiently.

The Materialist or Pleasure-seeker

In general, this is the practice of disregarding obligations to others with whom we relate in order to pursue individual interest or pleasure. An example would be a person who gets a divorce solely for the reason of marrying a much younger, more attractive partner. His/her action is not morally neutral because it has consequences for others with whom s/he has formed ties.

The Therapist

In general, people today have a much better standard of living compared to past generations. Even though this is the case, many people are not happy. Discontent and mild depression are common. A practice has arisen for people to go into therapy for treatment for their unhappiness. MacIntyre sees this as a symptom of people's preoccupation with themselves and their own needs. In addition, through therapy people may be encouraged to give even more attention to themselves and their needs. People do, of course, have psychological and related difficulties for which they need therapeutic help, and he acknowledges this. However, what people who are unhappy often need to do is recover the realisation that their happiness is achieved in and through engaging with others as members of a community. This, in turn, means they need to see that they can only become happy through practising virtues such as honesty, loyalty and compassion since such virtues sustain beneficial social engagement.

Taylor also refers to the emphasis individuals now place on satisfying their own needs, supported by therapy when needed (1989: 508).

Emotivism and Breakdown in Trust

One effect of the emotivist attitude is that, in the absence of shared ethical understanding, people compete with each other to have their point of view accepted. Each person sees himself/herself as a separate, isolated individual entitled to his/her own views and desires and determined to get them accepted and met. Where they conflict with the individual's viewpoint, judgments and advice about right or wrong have lost their power to be valid for him/her since s/he considers as morally valid only what s/he wants. Since we know that other people are trying to suit themselves, just as we are, this leads to people distrusting each other.

MacIntyre goes so far as to claim that the emotivist attitude leads to people trying to manipulate each other to get their way. In the absence of an accepted common social basis for ethics, we find no way open to us to project our own viewpoint 'except by directing toward others those very manipulative modes of relationship which we try to resist others imposing on us' (68).

At the same time, MacIntyre points out that we still use moral language to appeal to others to behave in ways we consider acceptable. We make statements such as 'You ought not to do that' or 'That is morally wrong' all the time. But the problem is that, having lost touch with a common basis in our human nature as social beings to which these statements could refer, such appeals are often ineffectual.

HUMAN NATURE AND OBTAINING THE GOODS OF SOCIAL PRACTICES

For MacIntyre, a necessary part of the solution to social problems lies in recognising that there is such a thing as moral authority. It lies in our human nature as social beings for which we need to practise the virtues, both for our own good and for the good of society. This provides a common basis for ethics (54–5).

THE NEED FOR VIRTUES

MacIntyre argues that by behaving in accordance with an emotivist attitude, we are hurting ourselves as much as others. The emotivist attitude prevents us from obtaining the good things that are available to us when we engage with others in social practices.

To illustrate why we need to behave virtuously if we are to obtain the goods of social practices, MacIntyre uses the example of the social practice of a child playing a game of chess. To obtain the goods internal to chess, a child needs to play honestly and not cheat. By playing honestly, the child develops certain capacities which are goods in the sense of being beneficial to him/her for his/her fulfilment in life and also beneficial for the community to which s/he belongs. MacIntyre identifies three goods internal to the social practice of chess:

- Analytic skill, i.e. being able to break down a situation or problem into the component parts in order to work out the best response to it.
- Strategic imagination, i.e. being able to plan ahead to achieve a desirable goal.
- Competitive intensity, i.e. being able to stand up to a challenge or adversity and to do one's best to overcome it.

To these internal, self-development goods can be added the satisfaction that comes from having tried to do one's best and from the social enjoyment of the game. We can see that they are real goods. By having them, people benefit themselves and each other. They are internal goods which enable a person to live well in managing life's demands and opportunities. The important point here is that these goods are only obtainable provided a person plays honestly and does not cheat. The person who cheats may get the external good of winning, but s/he is ultimately defeating himself/herself by losing out on the internal goods (188). The same can be said of the sportsperson or the businessperson who cheats in the social practice of sport and business. Trust, for example, is central to business. If investors cannot trust that companies are trustworthy, they will be less inclined to invest. This will result in a slowdown in economic growth, growth that provides the goods of employment for people and tax revenue for government to use for the well-being of society. This point was emphasised in 2002 at the time of the WorldCom and Enron corporate business scandals in the US in which billions of dollars were lost to investors and to people's pension funds.

In a similar way, goods internal to the social practice of family life include a feeling of belonging (in contrast, perhaps, to loneliness and isolation) as well as feelings of security and solidarity. To obtain such goods, the practice of the virtues of loyalty and helping out are necessary. We forfeit such goods through being uncaring and selfish in our family relationships. MacIntyre is not just arguing that there is a simple payback from practising the virtues. On a more fundamental level, he is arguing, as Aristotle did, that of themselves virtues provide us with the good life.

DEFINITION OF VIRTUE

MacIntyre gives the following definition of virtue:

A virtue is an acquired human quality the possession and exercise of which tends to enable us to achieve those goods which are internal to practices and the lack of which effectively prevents us from achieving any such goods.

MacIntyre 1985: 191

CORE VIRTUES

MacIntyre points to three core virtues needed to obtain the internal goods of any social practice. They are:

1. Justice, i.e. giving others their due in our relationship with them, e.g. recognising the part they play in the success of the practice; in particular it means recognising that we learn from them.
2. Courage, i.e. taking on the challenges, demands and risks of the practice.
3. Honesty, i.e. facing the facts and not overlooking awkward ones that are inconvenient. Honesty includes self-honesty in not deceiving ourselves about efforts needed to improve.

Without such virtues, engaging in social practices is 'pointless except as a device for achieving external goods' (191). He has no objection to external goods. External goods such as money and property are perfectly valid goods. They are natural objects of human desire. He says no one can despise them without being hypocritical. In addition, the wealthier we (and society) become, the more we are able to be effective in practising certain virtues such as generosity and justice (196). However, if external goods are obtained dishonestly, then a person cuts himself/herself off from internal goods.

SOCIAL PRACTICES, INSTITUTIONS AND MORAL CHALLENGE

No social practice can survive for any length of time without being institution-alised to some degree. Institutions such as sports clubs, business organisations and churches emerge to promote the practices of sport, business and worship. MacIntyre points out that because of their nature, institutions are characterised by power, status, competitiveness and acquisitiveness (194). As a result, members can come under pressure to give priority to maintaining and furthering the institution's power and status. In particular, they may try to protect the institution's reputation from scandal. When this happens they are no longer guided by virtues such as fairness, honesty and accountability. 'In this context the essential function of the virtues is clear: without them, without justice, courage and truthfulness, practices could not resist the corrupting power of institutions' (194).

NARRATIVE ETHICS

MacIntyre's ethics is also known for being an example of what is called *narrative ethics*. Narrative ethics has particular relevance as a guiding approach to assess and justify the care needs of individual clients. Narrative ethics places ethics in the context of each person's life considered as an individual's story. It is the story of the difficulties, challenges and opportunities life has given us and how we have responded to them. This ethics is based on the recognition of our intentions as the driving force in our life. We intend to do this or that and try to accomplish our intentions as best we can within our circumstances. In this way, we project ourselves into our future. We have intentions for both the short term, such as to get through the day or week by doing certain things, or for the long term, such as to get a job or see the world, or to live our whole life in a particular way (206–208). By the way we live out our intentions we become identified by the story of our life, both to ourselves and to others. We have a narrative identity that makes sense to us only because of its relation to the stories of others in the community (221; 223). Also, in this way, for MacIntyre our community or society and its well-being is closely bound up with our own identity.

What should guide our intentions if they are to be morally good? For MacIntyre, it is (no surprise!) the virtues. We give our life its pattern by how well or how badly we practise virtues such as self-honesty and courage (145). We also form our character (124). The more we practise virtues with constancy and integrity, the ethically stronger the narrative structure of our life becomes (203). Looking on narrative ethics from a social care perspective, we can recognise how clients may have come up against great obstacles in being able to shape their narrative. For example, care workers sometimes care for clients who have had a traumatic past and face a challenging future. This can be the case with asylum seekers, for example, and with unaccompanied minors, who in some cases could have fled a war zone and witnessed their parents being killed. It is clearly important for care workers to assess and provide for their needs by learning their individual stories. For example, they may need professional counselling. Narrative ethics points toward understanding people in the full light of their circumstances. It also points us toward the value of nurturing virtues, such as courage, in clients who may need it in order to cope.

Social Care and the Value of Social Well-being

For MacIntyre, social well-being requires people to practise the virtues in order to benefit from social practices. Virtues need to guide not only the activities of individuals and institutions, but also public policy. One traditional social practice has been the concern and care for the welfare of members who have difficulty meeting their own needs. In simple terms, providing a helping hand has always been central to the social fabric. It is a social practice from which everyone benefits in different ways and at different times. Apart from the benefit of receiving practical assistance, there are the benefits of living in a society with fewer and less serious social problems and with strong community ties. For everyone to benefit from concern and care for others requires recognition that behaviour needs to be informed by the practice of such virtues as compassion, justice and courage.

For the social care advocate, this understanding of social well-being can help justify the case for more state provision of services for those in need. Of particular relevance is MacIntyre's point that arguments which emphasise certain action, or lack of action, on the basis of economic considerations are not morally neutral because they can have direct implications for the well-being of others. This point of view supports the social care advocate's argument that economic considerations to do with lack of funding should not necessarily hold sway over a moral requirement to provide for care needs, and that providing for those needs strengthens the public good understood as social well-being. Also, as we saw in the previous section, social well-being for MacIntyre includes an understanding of ethics centred on the unique narrative of each person's life. This supports a client-centred, empathetic approach to care.

Question for Consideration and Discussion: Does Irish Society Suffer from 'Moral Poverty'?

With the development of the *Celtic Tiger* economy which has seen Ireland grow, in a short period, from a relatively poor country up until the end of the 1980s to one of the richest by the end of the 1990s, social commentators have pointed out that it has brought with it a decline in practising moral values, which has had a detrimental effect on society. Consider whether Irish society suffers from moral poverty in the light of the following extract from Ombudsman Emily O'Reilly's address to the annual Céifin conference in 2004, and in the light of MacIntyre's view of the value of social well-being and of the practice of virtues to achieve it. Emily O'Reilly appreciates the many benefits that prosperity has brought, especially for those who would otherwise be poor. At the same time she recoils from

> . . . the vulgar fest that is much of modern Ireland, the rampant, unrestrained drunkenness, the brutal, random violence that infects the smallest of our townlands and villages, the incontinent use of foul language with no thought to place or company, the obscene parading of obscene wealth, the debasement of our civic life, the growing disdain of the wealthy toward the poor, the fracturing of our community life.

She sees the ethical root for this in 'a moral poverty' where we are 'increasingly neutral in our judgments of all sorts of objectively bad behaviour'. (For her full address, which is well worth reading for one person's snapshot of Irish society, see www.charleville.com/food.)

CRITICAL EVALUATION OF MACINTYRE'S VIRTUE THEORY

Virtue Versus Personal Freedom

MacIntyre is credited with reviving recognition that virtues are not just for *do-gooders*, but are a social necessity. Without them, individual fulfilment, which is bound up with social engagement, will suffer. So, too, will the public good, since without the recognition of the social necessity of virtue, people will be pulling against each other to get their preferences met rather than with each other to achieve their fulfilment as social beings.

At the same time, it can be argued that MacIntyre underestimates the value of personal freedom. Some people argue that making a success of their plans and activities or talents enables them to lead fulfilling lives. They may accept that society needs people to be virtuous, but not that it is central to personal fulfilment. This idea of the autonomous individual doing his/her *own thing*, the idea of what is called *expressive individualism*, is well-established in our society as an operative value for many. At the same time, this value co-exists in varying degrees of influence in guiding behaviour with the value of concern and care for others, in particular for family and friends.

Also, personal freedom is a crucial value in enabling people to act against restrictive social practices that are the norm. By emphasising the need for virtue to maintain social practices, there is the danger that the virtues may act to prolong existing practices that are unjustified. For example, if women had not criticised the social practices that required them to be subordinate to men and, instead, remained in an inferior economic and social position through the practice of such virtues as obedience, loyalty and humility expected at the time, the unjust social practice would not have been challenged, at least not to the same extent. It is partly through giving value to the desire for personal freedom that moral change occurs, often against much initial opposition from society, but which in retrospect is regarded as having been valid and necessary. MacIntyre is not arguing against the value of personal freedom or against the necessity for changing unjust social practices. However, there is a tension in his account between practising the virtues to benefit from the goods of social practices and practising them to change those practices where change is justified.

REVIEW

An individualist ethics is understandable in giving more power and authority to people to make up their own minds about what values they want to have. However, there is a danger that it will lead to people suiting themselves and losing touch with their social nature, as well as with the need to practise virtues to obtain the benefits of social practices.

FURTHER READING

O'Reilly, E. (2004) 'Imagining the Future – An Irish Perspective'.
   www.charleville.com/food
See also the Céifin Centre for Values-led Change at www.ceifin.com.

REFERENCES

MacIntyre, A. (1985) *After Virtue*, Duckworth.
Taylor, C. (1989) *Sources of the Self: The Making of the Modern Identity*, Cambridge
   University Press.
www.americanrhetoric.com (click on 'Movie Speeches' then 'Wall Street').

10
Social Contract Ethics

OVERALL AIM

To explore ethical reasons that influence the overall direction of social policy in two different viewpoints about what constitutes the agreed good.

LEARNING OUTCOMES

At the end of this chapter you should be able to:

- Give an account of how Hobbes's contract and Rousseau's derive from their view of people in a state of nature.
- For each contract, show how particular ethical requirements follow, requirements which inform the purpose and direction of social policy.
- Connect the ethical requirements for peace, security and individual self-interest under Hobbes's social contract with conservative or neo-liberal social policies.
- Connect the requirements for freedom, equality and common interest under Rousseau's contract with labour or social democratic social policies.
- Evaluate the merits and weaknesses of the ideas behind each contract in their influence on the direction of social policy.

INTRODUCTION

Social care work takes place in the context of social conditions that exist in society, and care workers constantly come up against these conditions in providing care. These conditions can restrict or facilitate people's care needs. There is a range of such conditions relating, for example, to levels of wealth and poverty in society and employment and educational opportunities. There are more specific conditions such as eligibility for social housing and housing waiting lists, and availability of developmental services for people with learning challenges.

One set of ethics which influences the viewpoint people have toward social conditions is known as social contract ethics. Social contract ethics places emphasis on people's membership of society. It is our membership of society, these theories claim, which is the most important thing about us when it comes to understanding ethical requirements.

What constitutes the social good has been the subject of much debate over the centuries. This debate is about the big question of the purpose of society. One way of addressing the question is to ask, 'What does everyone agree the good should be which they want the state to help them to achieve in the way it relates to them?' As we shall see, the question has been answered in two basic and contrasting ways. These two ways gave rise to the idea of two different types of contract between the people and the state, with each having different implications for the kind of social policies that will provide for the social good.

Hobbes (1588–1679) claims that, if we were asked, we would want the state to provide us with peace and security and the conditions to pursue our own self-interest as much as possible. Since these are the things we would want first and foremost, they should inform and direct the government's policies. Also, Hobbes claims we would all agree on this, and so it forms the basis for a contract between ourselves and the government. Rousseau (1712–78), in contrast, claims that, if we were asked, we would want the government to provide us with freedom and equality above all, and we would want them to provide for the common interest more than our individual self-interest. Rousseau, too, claims we would agree on this and so it should form the basis of a contract between ourselves and the government.

The ideas in each contract have had a big influence on understanding the role of political rule in providing for the social good and they continue to have influence. From Hobbes's contract comes the idea that the state has little requirement to provide directly for the welfare needs of citizens. This view stresses that individuals have responsibility for providing for their own needs. Broadly speaking, in politics, this is the view which conservatives or neo-liberals take to a greater or lesser extent to justify their social policies. From Rousseau's social contract, on the other hand, comes the idea that the state has a large responsibility to provide directly for the welfare needs of all citizens. Generally, in politics, this is the view that lies behind socialist, social democratic and labour social policies to a greater or lesser extent. It's important to emphasise that neither type of party bases its social policy directly on the ideas of Hobbes or Rousseau. In addition, party members would not necessarily agree with their ideas. The ideas are only one broad, background influence that has contributed to what is called a party's *ideology*. A number of other ideas from political theory also exert influence. Also, in practice, the policies of the different parties can differ in important respects from what Hobbes's and Rousseau's ideas suggest. This is due partly to the demands of practical politics, in particular to the influence of social conditions that prevail at a given time and the influence of the views of the public. At the same time, the parties can be considered to be guided broadly by the two different perspectives which the ideas provide.

HYPOTHETICAL NATURE OF THE SOCIAL CONTRACT

The first thing to make clear about the social contract is that there never has been an actual contract, nor is there ever likely to be one. The idea is hypothetical. It is supposed or imagined – but for a very real purpose. This purpose is to understand what type of public good people would sign up for in a contract so that it could then be provided for in reality. Ideas we find convincing – and thereby win our agreement – form the basis of the contract, which justifies it as a guide to social policy.

HOBBES'S SOCIAL CONTRACT

The Desire for Power

Hobbes accepts a basic moral relativism as his starting point. Arising from it he will show:

- Why we need a social contract.
- What the contract should provide.

Hobbes's moral relativism is one that takes a bleak view of human nature, but some would say it is realistic. He holds that in reality, no actions are good or bad in themselves, nor are there any common rules about how people should relate to good and bad. Instead, good is simply whatever a person instinctively desires and bad is whatever s/he instinctively has an aversion for (1968: 120). There is nothing else to good and bad other than a perpetual seeking to satisfy desires. It is the meaning of happiness (129–30).

In trying to satisfy his/her desires, each person acts in isolation from others, looking after himself/herself first and foremost. This gives rise to competition and conflict over the means of satisfying desires. As a result, a person desires power above all in order to be able to hold onto and increase his capacity to satisfy his desires. 'I put it for a general inclination of all mankind, a perpetual and restless desire for power after power, that ceases only in death' (161).

State of Nature

Hobbes imagines what life would be like in a state of nature where there is no *common power* in the form of society as we know it and, in particular, no enforceable laws. Life in a state of nature would be 'a war of every man against every man' (188). He is not saying that people would actually be engaged in physical aggression and defence all the time, although he believes it would be common. He includes in his idea of war the fear of aggression, which he believes would be constant. It is fear from knowing that people will of their nature attack you if they feel they need to in satisfying their desires (185–6).

In this state of nature there are no common conveniences because they require co-operation and people do not co-operate – there is no industry, no culture and only 'a continual fear, and danger of violent death'. Hobbes follows this with a description of life that has often been quoted since, though it is sometimes forgotten that he is referring not to life as it is in society, but only to how it would be in a state of nature. He says that in a state of nature 'the life of man' is 'solitary, poor, nasty, brutish, and short' (186). He accepts that this never was the actual condition for all mankind, but believes that it would have been for some peoples at certain times and that in his time it continued to be in some places (187).

For Hobbes this is the type of behaviour people exhibit because of their nature. He is not decrying it or deploring it. He is simply accepting it as the reality on which any view of social good will have to be based if it is to win agreement.

From the State of Nature to the Social Contract

Hobbes then points out that living in a climate of fear and aggression is to no one's advantage. This is because he believes people are roughly equal in strength of mind and body, so no one will really be able to gain at the expense of others through force. In any event, those who do succeed will still always be in fear of having whatever advantages they acquire taken from them by others who are weaker but who combine forces (183). In other words, a state of nature is not a state conducive to *anyone* being able to satisfy their desires because they need peace and security to do so. This is why the idea of a social contract for the whole of society arises. Through a social contract, people look to society to protect them. 'Fear of oppression disposes a man . . . to seek aid from society: for there is no other way by which a man can secure his life and liberty' (163). Put simply, a contract makes good sense. It is prudent.

The Social Contract

In a state of nature each person has a *right of nature* to use his own power to do whatever it takes to preserve his own life. Self-preservation is an absolutely fundamental right. So, under the contract, people agree to transfer this natural right to look after their own self-preservation to a ruler, for the purpose of peace and security. Each person gives up that amount of his natural liberty as is necessary to ensure peace (189–90). It is this 'mutual transferring of Right' to the state which gives rise to the social contract (192). Since we transfer our right to preserve our own life to the state, it then becomes the main job of the state to protect our lives for us. It becomes the job of the state to protect everyone through laws and their enforcement so we can all go about our business in peace and security. This, for Hobbes, is the only item in the contract because it is the only item on which people would be sure to agree. We can see, then, how it follows from this contract that the state has only this limited or minimal role of providing for whatever is necessary to maintain the peace.

Historical Note

In Hobbes's time the sovereign or king had the power to provide peace and security. But, as you can imagine, the idea that the only justifiable society is one based on the agreement of all threatened the power of the king. Hobbes's idea was a force in history that led to modern democracy, which allows for a government to be elected by agreement.

Morality under the Contract

Morality under the contract relates solely to behaving in ways that maintain the peace. Thus, respect for the laws designed to provide for peace, and respect for the independence and freedom of everyone under the law, are high on the list of moral requirements.

Hobbes is sometimes represented as saying we have no moral obligations to others except the more negative one of refraining from harming them through observing the law, but he lists other, more positive requirements. They are an important part of his theory, but not often emphasised. These more positive requirements have for him the status of moral laws. He says we should treat everyone as equal and be fair in our dealings with them, as well as showing them gratitude and mercy. However, we should not do so because we know these are good ways to behave in themselves (we don't know that they are). Instead, we should practise these traditional virtues only because they help to avoid social conflict and provide for social harmony. There is no other reason or justification for them.

At the same time, Hobbes goes so far as to say that there is a moral requirement on the state to provide welfare for people under laws if through no fault of their own they are unable to work. Social welfare, at least for the unemployed, is a good thing. Assisting them should not be left to private charity alone. But, again, the only reason why the state should provide welfare is to avoid poverty becoming a cause of social conflict. Also, significantly for Hobbes, state welfare is charity. Welfare is not something due to people as of right for their self-preservation (387).

The crucial thing for Hobbes is that these moral laws are derived entirely from the recognition of the need for peace. They have no other foundation (216), and they have no other call on us either. Putting it another way, we invent morality as a rational response to conflict with others by identifying it with laws and practices that are in our own interest. Morality under the social contract is only a necessary device – a device to provide for what is called *enlightened* self-interest.

HOBBES'S ETHICS AND SOCIAL CARE

State's Limited Role

For Hobbes, the social contract provides understanding for the idea that the state is required to provide for the public or social good. However, the state's responsibility for the social good is limited to providing for peace and security for all. These are clearly basic and important care needs for everyone but people have many other care needs besides peace and security, however broadly peace and security needs may be interpreted. For example, people in poverty need care whether or not their condition will give rise to some of them becoming a threat to social order through using force as a political means or by engaging in anti-social behaviour.

Furthermore, the reason the state's power is limited to providing peace and security is to allow us the most freedom possible to pursue our own self-interest, to which we have a natural right, since this is how we would behave in a state of nature. This gives rise to a society characterised by *possessive individualism* whereby each individual seeks to advance his own interests (MacPherson 1962).

Political and Social Policy Implications

In politics, conservatives generally, and neo-liberals in particular, take the view that a small, limited role for the state in providing for people's care needs through social welfare is the most that is justified. They maintain that individuals have a natural right to do what they want for themselves without interference by the state. Thus they argue that low taxes and low spending to provide for care needs are justified for the sake of supporting both the right and responsibility of individuals to look after themselves.

Also, conservatives and neo-liberals today usually make the economic argument that self-interest is the driving force for creating a wealthy society, which ends up not just being for the benefit of a few, but for the benefit of all. They point out that if the state puts curbs on individual freedom through high taxation, then this creates disincentives for individuals to use their freedom to pursue their self-interest in creating wealth, with the result that society as a whole suffers from lack of wealth creation. They argue that to provide the maximum incentive to work is the best way of ensuring wealth will be created, wealth that will then spread to others through its owners investing it productively to create more wealth, thereby leading to a need for more people to be employed. This is the *rising tide lifts all boats* argument. It is also sometimes called *the trickle down effect*.

In addition, if a society is doing well economically, then even with low taxes the government will be getting a bigger tax take than otherwise. This means it will have more money to spend on care services if it chooses to do so. In this way conservatives and neo-liberals might argue that their approach can lead to the means to provide for more and better care services. At the same time, they believe in the value of providing for self-interest more than in the state providing people with services, so it's debatable whether their approach does in fact provide the best prospect of care for everyone. A labour or social democratic view would say it doesn't because without state assistance, a considerable minority loses out in relation to the rest of society. Therefore, they argue that the state needs to spend a lot on providing directly for their care needs.

A Divided Society

Critics have questioned Hobbes's basic point that there is an equality of strength between people. In reality, people differ considerably in their levels of both physical and mental capacity. This means a contract which provides for only the limited social good of everybody's physical security suits those who will not need social care more than it suits those who will need it. It will certainly not suit people who have a disability or mental illness. Also, because of the overriding importance Hobbes places on a right to self-preservation, as long as people are not endangering the peace, there is nothing to restrict them from pursuing their self-interest to become wealthy and powerful, if they so desire, and then using their position to maintain and increase their advantage with little obligation to others.

Morality as Mutual Convenience and Charity

In Hobbes's ethics care is provided either for the practical reason of helping to hold society together or out of charity. It is not required from a sense of justice as something good in itself. In practice, therefore, state services for people in need will always be insecure and uncertain. They will depend either on the charitable disposition of rulers or on their judgment about the extent to which poverty may be a threat to social order.

ROUSSEAU'S SOCIAL CONTRACT

People in the State of Nature

In contrast to Hobbes's view of how human beings would behave in a state of nature, Rousseau believed people would have had a natural sympathy toward each other. In addition to looking out for themselves, they would have recognised that hardship was common. Particularly in the early stages of emergence from a state of nature into social organisation, the need to provide for basic necessities as well as coping with illnesses and natural disasters would have nurtured in people a spirit of co-operation and mutual aid (Cranston 1972: 20–21).

At the same time, life in Rousseau's state of nature is *precarious and uncertain*. This is because if other people tried to take advantage of us, we would need *physical strength* to defend our freedom and possessions. Also, in a state of nature people are not so much free as independent and separated from each other (Rousseau 1972: 77), so it's no ideal state. Only by forming into society can we fully realise our freedom by uniting with each other for our mutual benefit. If we want to be free, we have to join with others in following rules for our own good and the good of others. Ethics arises fully in the need to establish rules and abide by them (64–5).

Rousseau's Criticism of How Society Developed

The problem, as Rousseau sees it, is that the way society developed did not lead to freedom for everyone. This is expressed in the famous opening two sentences from *The Social Contract*: 'Man was born free, and he is everywhere in chains. Those who think themselves the masters of others are indeed greater slaves than they' (49).

How did conditions in which people lack freedom come about? Rousseau says it came about through competition among people for possessions and power, in particular through people acquiring and increasing ownership of property. This did not lead to freedom and equality, but to restriction and inequality. It led to a society in which there was a class division between rich and poor. It led to inequality and exploitation, which in turn led to both the threat, and occurrence, of civil disturbance and violence. It led to a society in which even the wealthy and powerful still had to fear for the security of their possessions and position. (This explains his point that 'masters' are still 'slaves'.) Rousseau makes two interrelated points about this society.

His first point is that such a society is in nobody's best interest. His second point is that it is unjust because it came about without agreement. Therefore an agreement between people, or a social contract, is needed to provide a morally justifiable basis for society that will be in everyone's interest. 'Since no man has any natural authority over his fellows, and since force alone bestows no right, all legitimate authority among men must be based on covenants' (53).

Rousseau's Contract

Freedom and Democracy

Rousseau says that the social contract is essentially about building on the natural independence we had in a state of nature in order to provide for real freedom. It is about having a form of social organisation in which natural independence is furthered or developed through being converted into social or civic freedom. In drawing up the contract, the task is

> . . . to find a form of association which will defend the person and goods of each member with the collective force of all, and under which each individual, while uniting himself with others, obeys no one but himself, and remains as free as before.
>
> Rousseau 1972: 60

A society in which people are free in this way is the only one we could envisage getting the agreement of everyone. Since a free person is one who rules himself/herself, so a free society is one in which the people make their own laws and rules which they then follow. In short, the social contract provides for a democratic society.

Historical Note

Rousseau's *The Social Contract* was one of the books which influenced the French Revolution, in which rule of the king was overthrown, to be replaced by democracy.

The Problem of Providing a True Democracy

Ideally the social contract should provide for a direct democracy, as distinct from a representative democracy in which the people elect politicians to represent them. A direct democracy is one in which all citizens would be directly involved in making the decisions. This is a true democracy. But Rousseau recognises that a direct democracy is not practical given the large number of citizens in a modern state (122). At the same time, he recognises that there is a problem with representative democracy. This is not only because, strictly speaking, people can only represent themselves, but because people will differ on the kind of laws they will want their representatives to introduce. The rich, for example, will want their representatives to introduce laws that favour their own interests, and so also will the poor. The result will be a struggle for power among different sections of society, with the section that succeeds in getting most representatives elected winning.

The 'General Will'

Rousseau's solution to the problem is his idea of the *general will*. The general will is different to the will of all. The will of all is the outcome of agreement about providing for everybody's private desires or interests, but the general will is the common interest (72). As he puts it, 'the general will derives its generality less from the number of voices than from the common interest which unites them' (76). In other words, the general will is a psychological bond that unites people, both in their humanity and need for social co-operation. It 'should spring from all and apply to all' (75). In practice, for those making decisions about what the general will means in a particular case, it is a matter of considering what best serves the interests of everyone as a whole.

> When a law is proposed in the people's assembly, what is asked of them is not whether they approve the proposition or reject it, but whether it is in conformity with the general will which is theirs; each by giving his vote gives his opinion on the question, and the counting of votes yields a declaration of the general will.
>
> Rousseau 1972: 153

What the general will means for a particular matter 'does not always have to be unanimous' (70). At the same time, 'the general will is always rightful and always leads toward the public good' (72).

Values Provided by the General Will: Freedom and Equality

The main value of the general will is to provide for the freedom of everybody. Decisions made about society have to provide for it as a priority. Also, because the general will relates to everybody, it has to relate to everybody equally. Thus, decisions made have to provide for everyone's freedom equally. Acts of the general will should 'make no distinction between any of the members who compose it' (76). Any form of discrimination is ruled out by the principle of providing for the general will.

Meaning of Equality in Living Standards

But what about differences between people in terms of the standard of living they can enjoy? By equality, Rousseau says he does not mean that everyone has to have the same income or standard of living. Equality for him means ensuring that there are no great differences in income between people. He says that in the interests of the general will, the rich should be moderate in their expectation of having wealth, and the poor should be moderate in desiring wealth.

Also, he is not strongly opposed to a society being made up of interest groups representing different sections of society. He seems to accept that interest groups are likely to occur in practice since people are inclined to look to the interests of the group to which they belong more so than the general interest. He says that if there are to be interest groups, there should be many of them so they can balance each other out in the level of influence they are able to exert (73–4). In these ways the general will can provide for a harmonious society (96).

ROUSSEAU'S CONTRACT AND SOCIAL CARE VALUES

State Provision of Measures to Meet Care Needs

The social good that follows from Rousseau's contract supports social care directly. This is shown in particular through his idea of equality. In practice, equality means ensuring that nobody is too poor or too rich. People are to have incomes close to each other. In line with this is the requirement that no group, whether older people or those with disability, should be at a disadvantage compared to the rest of society where the state is in a position to remove that disadvantage. Catering for the needs of disadvantaged groups through legal provision is in keeping with consideration of the general will, with the common bond that unites all people.

COMBINED INFLUENCE OF BOTH TYPES OF CONTRACT

In practice, some combination of the general perspective afforded by Hobbes's and Rousseau's ethical ideas for a social contract tends to influence the overall direction of social policy rather than one to the exclusion of the other. However, one more than the other will be emphasised and have more influence depending on the type of political party in power.

Exercise 10.1

Question for Consideration and Discussion: Families at Risk

Whose ideas, and related direction for social policy, Hobbes's or Rousseau's, do you think should inform the *vision* and *principles* referred to in the following report?

A report commissioned by the Irish government on family support services concluded that 'there is no overarching vision or set of principles driving the development of the services.' The effects of this are that 'health authorities are not meeting their statutory obligations to provide sufficient support to families and children at risk' in order to minimise 'social unrest and future communal problems'.

(Source: *Irish Times* editorial, 20 March 2006.)

Exercise 10.2

Question for Consideration and Discussion: No Such Thing as Society?

Consider Margaret Thatcher's view, expressed below, and relate it to both Hobbes's and Rousseau's ideas for the direction of social policy. Think of examples of particular social policies that follow from her view and those that would not follow from it.

> [The people constantly requesting government intervention] are casting their problems at society. And, as you know, there is no such thing as society. There are individual men, women and their families. And no government can do anything except through people, and people must look after themselves first. It is our duty to look after ourselves and then, also, to look after our neighbours.

Source: From an interview published in *Woman's Own*, 23 September 1987. Quote available online at http://wikiquote.org under 'Margaret Thatcher'.

CRITICAL EVALUATION OF HOBBES'S SOCIAL CONTRACT

No Actual Contract

One criticism that can easily be made is that there never was, nor is there ever likely to be, an actual social contract. Therefore the kind of contract people would agree to is, at best, only plausible speculation.

Unlikely to Win Agreement of All

Would Hobbes's contract be one which those in need of care would willingly agree to, since it makes them dependant on charity? Hardly. It won't serve their interests as equal members of society. The problem is that under Hobbes's theory people are seen as having only an equality of approximate strength. They are not accorded an equality of moral status. This is a point made by Kymlicka (2004: 189–91).

Contract Open to Being Broken

A problem with Hobbes's view is that, in practice, the need for peace and security is unlikely to provide *of itself* a sufficient moral reason to prevent people harming others. The thing about a contract is that it can be broken. People may well feel tempted to break it if they feel they can get away with it and avoid punishment. There is no other moral requirement stopping them, since morality is identified only with the contract.

Provides Justification for the Value of Individual Freedom

At the same time, Hobbes's contract supports the value of individual freedom. In other words, for him the common good, which the contract provides for, is precisely to allow for maximum individual freedom. It can also be argued that by facilitating individual freedom you are facilitating human nature, and that this is the best way of ensuring society will work for the benefit of all.

CRITICAL EVALUATION OF ROUSSEAU'S SOCIAL CONTRACT

Unrealistic View of Human Nature

We can see how Rousseau has a very different idea from Hobbes about how the social contract serves the social good. For Rousseau, the contract is not a practical necessity for our self-preservation so much as a moral requirement to underpin and provide for relations of freedom and equality among people. However, the main problem with Rousseau's social contract is making it work. It would seem to be expecting too much of people that they would set aside their private interests and be guided only by a notion of the general will.

Vagueness of the General Will

Freedom and equality can be expressed in tangible ways as manifestations of the general will, for example, by a minimum wage and high-quality social services. At the same time, the general will remains a vague notion. People have to look into their own souls, as it were, to see what is in the best interests of everyone. But this is quite a subjective process, and people could understandably reach different conclusions.

Contradiction in Forcing People to Be Free

There is the danger that an idea like the general will would be abused by some people if they attained power. There is a notorious passage in which Rousseau raises the question of what is to happen to a person who refuses to obey the general will. His answer is that in the interests of ensuring that the will has force, such a person 'shall be constrained to do so by the whole body, which means nothing other than that he shall be forced to be free' (64). Putting it another way, people are not allowed to live in accordance with their own good, as they see it, where it differs from the general will. They have to be made to comply with the requirements of the general will. This, as you can imagine, could easily lead to the suppression of people's individual freedom.

Rousseau himself is not advocating any form of tyranny. As we have seen, individual freedom is, for him, of the first importance. However, in order to try to secure freedom in society for everyone, he ends up suggesting that the freedom to be different can be suppressed where it is not in accordance with the rulers' interpretation of general will. Furthermore, in history, his idea of the authority of the general will has provided justification for others, who believed they knew what the general will was, to impose laws on the people restricting their freedom. It has been done in the name of the *general will* or the *common good* or simply *the people*. This happened in the twentieth century, particularly in the totalitarian communist states of the former Soviet Union. However, this form of state rule was influenced much more by the ideas of Karl Marx.

Brief Note on Marx's Ideas

Marx argued that the structure of the capitalist economic system inevitably gives rise to injustice and oppression for a section of society that has little capital and power. Those who own a lot of capital use their wealth to ensure the political process and public policy maintains and increases their advantage over those who own little. Marx's solution involved public ownership and control of resources, property and production of goods and services in the interest of providing a just society for all. With the collapse of the communist system in the former Soviet Union and countries of Eastern Europe at the end of the 1980s, Marx's ideas lost much of their influence.

REVIEW

Social contract ethics is about the social good that follows from regarding society as based on an agreement between members. Two different types of contract have been put forward as justified, with different views following from each about what the social good requires by way of social policy. Under Hobbes's contract the state provides for peace and security so that people can pursue their own self-interest as they choose. Under Rousseau's contract the state provides for the general will, understood as the freedom and equality of all in practical terms such as material well-being in the common interest. Hobbes's type of contract represents one broad background influence on the social policy of conservative or neo-liberal parties and Rousseau's on the policy of labour or social democratic parties.

FURTHER READING

Benn, P. (1998) *Ethics*, UCL Press (Chapter 5).

REFERENCES

Hobbes, T. (1968) *Leviathan*, Pelican Classics.

Kymlicka, W. (2004) 'The Social Contract Tradition' in *A Companion to Ethics*, P. Singer (ed.), Blackwell.

MacPherson, C. (1962), *The Political Theory of Possessive Individualism: Hobbes to Locke*, Oxford University Press.

Rousseau, J. (1972) *The Social Contract*, Penguin Classics.

11
Social Justice

OVERALL AIM

To explore the key role that ideas of social justice play in providing social care.

LEARNING OUTCOMES

At the end of this chapter you should be able to:

• Relate the idea of justice to the idea of rights.
• Explain Aristotle's 'right proportion' understanding of social justice.
• Explain Rawls's understanding of social justice as fairness.
• Explain Nozick's entitlement understanding.
• Relate each idea of social justice to social care policy provisions.
• Support the idea of social justice for clients on the basis of an informed viewpoint that takes account of different ways social justice is understood.

INTRODUCTION

Justice is a powerful idea. Injustice arouses strong feelings. People have fought and died to achieve what they believed to be justice. Mill says the reason why people are so affected by justice is that it bears directly on their means of survival and security. They feel it is something they cannot be without. This is why demands for justice are seen as the strongest of ethical demands. The feeling is not merely that justice *ought* to be provided, but that it *must* be (Mill 1944: 50–51).

Justice is something people feel should lie at the foundation of their relationship with each other, at the foundation of their society, and indeed at the foundation of the world's economic and social order. But what exactly is it? As we shall see in considering the theories of Rawls and Nozick, some people can see certain economic and social conditions as just, while others see the same conditions as unjust. People dispute what justice means in practice. Arising from different ideas of what social justice means are different implications for the kind of polices that serve justice. Mill identified three general features which people associate with justice.

Moral Right

The easiest way to identify features of justice is to look at why some conditions are regarded as unjust. For Mill, injustice is either withholding from people, or taking away from them, something to which they have a moral right (41). Also, we say that justice is something which people *deserve*. So, social justice is something people *deserve as of right*.

Legal Entitlement

Justice is also connected with law (44). If certain social arrangements are considered just and deserved as of right, then people expect that they will be provided for in law. This puts the provision of justice on a much stronger footing than, say, generosity. We don't say of people that they have a right to generosity, let alone a legal entitlement to it (46) – but we do say this of justice.

Equality

But what kinds of things do we have a right to expect from society as a matter of justice? First and foremost, justice relates to the right to be treated equally. For example, it relates to the right to be treated equally under the law. Equal pay for equal work regardless of gender or ethnicity is another example of justice as equality. In general, if people are being treated less favourably than others for no good reason, then we say they are being treated unjustly. Care workers may come across cases where some children in a family are being treated less favourably than others, perhaps because of disability or gender.

SOCIAL JUSTICE

This relates to the overall arrangements that should be provided for people in terms of their living standards. The first view holds that there should be a relatively equal arrangement of wealth in the interests of the common good. The implication of this first view is that the wealth in society should be shared out or distributed. The second view holds that a just arrangement of wealth is one in which people provide for themselves. The implication of this second view is that people are entitled to keep the wealth they acquire; for some this view includes the idea that it is unjust for wealth to be taken off people through tax and given to others in welfare payments and free or subsidised public services.

Aristotle and Rawls argue, for different reasons, that for the state to provide a greater level of equality in living standards is morally just and Nozick argues that it is morally unjust.

ARISTOTLE'S VIEW: SOCIAL JUSTICE AS BALANCE

For Aristotle, justice is a key virtue because the just person is constantly disposed toward the good, not merely toward himself/herself, but at the same time toward others. For him social justice refers to the way money or other material benefits should be divided or distributed among members of a community. Remember, a virtue for Aristotle is the midpoint between extremes of excess and deficiency. This means that an unjust society and world is where there is extreme wealth alongside extreme poverty. Social justice is the mean between these extremes. In practice, this requires providing for a greater level of equality in living standards with no big gap between those who are rich and those who are poor by comparison. The just is *a right proportion* or balance, and the unjust is a violation of that proportion (1955: 144–7). The traditional emblem of justice, weighing scales in balance, expresses this idea. Broadly speaking, the *right proportion* is judged on what people deserve in terms of their contribution to society, and in terms of the needs they have for which they may require assistance if they are to achieve well-being. So you can argue, for example, it is just to apply a higher rate of tax on incomes above a certain level since people on such incomes have more than provided for their own needs, while at the same time it would be unjust to tax them unduly given their efforts. Also, you can argue that those who are unable to provide for their own needs deserve, in justice, that society provides for them.

Aristotle accepts that, in practice, it is difficult for anyone to judge precisely what the right proportion is that people deserve to have. But he maintains it is an essential pubic task and virtue which people (public leaders especially) should practise. A just society and world are ones in which everybody can flourish.

Aristotle also wrote an influential book called *Politics*. In his *Ethics* he points out that political activity has greater importance in contributing to the flourishing of everybody than people's individual efforts (1955: 27). The main way that politics does this is through an elected government having the power to redistribute the wealth of society justly from the money it raises in tax.

ARISTOTLE'S SOCIAL JUSTICE AND SOCIAL CARE

Aristotle's meaning of social justice is probably the one that accords with most people's understanding. That is, a just society and world is one in which there is no big gap between rich and poor. Governments are frequently criticised for being unjust where their policies result in widening the gap. In particular, budget welfare increases and tax reductions can be judged on the basis of their net overall effect on narrowing or widening the income gap between welfare recipients, or those on low pay, and high earners.

Also, through growing the economy to provide jobs and especially through having a National Anti-Poverty Strategy (NAPS), introduced in 1997, the government can be regarded as seeking to provide for greater justice in Aristotle's sense. Setting targets for poverty reduction is one element of the anti-poverty strategy. The strategy also obliges each government department to consider the effect of its policies to ensure that they contribute to reducing poverty rather than increasing it. These are the kinds of measure which, if taken seriously, fit in with what Aristotle understands it means to provide social justice.

RAWLS'S VIEW OF SOCIAL JUSTICE AS FAIRNESS

The Veil of Ignorance Condition

Rawls argues that it is only fair that we decide on the principles of justice from behind 'a veil of ignorance'. This means we must imagine we know nothing about ourselves, neither about our economic or social status, nor our abilities and talents. There is a complete blackout on such knowledge. We should not ask, 'What principle of justice would I adopt if I knew what my talents, interests and station in life would be?' Instead we should ask, 'What principle of justice would I adopt if I were ignorant of my talents, interests and station in life?' (Rawls 2004: 514).

In deciding on social justice 'it is essential that no one knows his place in society, his class position or social status. Nor does any one know his future in the distribution of natural assets or abilities, his intelligence, strength and the like' (514). The veil requires us to assume we have no way of understanding in advance what sort of person we are or our place in society.

The veil returns us to 'the original position'. This is not some real original position which either we or our ancestors were ever in – it is purely imaginary or hypothetical. Rawls's purpose in asking us to go there in our mind is very practical. It is so we can decide on principles of justice that will be fair because we will all be deciding on them from the same position. They will be fair because we will all decide on them 'in a situation of equality'. In other words, the veil forces us to be fair. This is the reason he calls his theory 'justice as fairness' (515).

But what's the point, you may still ask, in going there in our mind if it never existed in reality and never will? Rawls's answer to this objection is that the conditions of fairness presented in the original position are 'ones which we do in fact accept' as fair. 'Or, if we do not, then perhaps we can be persuaded to do so by philosophical reflection' (519).

Two Further Reasons for Employing the Veil Condition

Necessary for Agreement on Principles

Without the veil, Rawls argues we have no chance of ever getting agreement on principles of justice. This is because those who are wealthy will want to hold onto their wealth, while those who are poor will want to improve their position through society giving them more benefits. Since the wealthy will regard the money they make as their own, they will select a principle that regards it as unjust for them to have to pay taxes to support those on welfare. Those on welfare, on the other hand, will feel entitled to regard it as just that the wealthy contribute to their welfare by arguing, for example, that since everyone is a member of society by birth they are entitled to a decent share of society's wealth. By getting rid of bias (we would need to know our actual position to be biased), the veil makes possible agreement on principles of justice which provide for everyone's interest (518).

Minimises the Influence of Luck

As things stand, luck plays a huge part in influencing a person's prospects in life. This is because so much depends on the circumstances we are born into, which are a matter of luck or 'natural chance' (514). We could be born the son or daughter of wealthy, caring and happy parents, or of parents mired in poverty and personal problems. However, using the veil condition means that our position will not depend so much on luck, but on the arrangements agreed by everyone for everyone. These arrangements will be, as we shall see in the next section, to provide for the best possible position for everyone.

The Veil Condition Provides for 'A Natural Lottery'

Deciding on principles of justice behind the veil can be described as playing *a natural lottery*. Imagine all the positions in society as slips of paper in a lottery drum. Before the drum is twirled and we pick out a slip, we are given the opportunity to write on a slip the kind of position we would like to have. Nothing could be fairer. So what kind of position will we write on the slip?

Rawls argues that the position we would write coincides with what is rational and, because it is rational, it is just. In general terms we would want the best possible position for ourselves. This is a rational choice. It is not just our choice, it is everyone's rational choice. So what, then, does *best possible position* mean in practice as the rational choice? He says that rationally we would want to choose two things for this position, and that as a result of these two things there are two principles of justice.

The Type of Position We Would Choose

Civil Liberties

Our first choice, he says, would be to have the maximum amount of individual freedom. Without freedom, some people would have power over others without their consent – no one would want to choose this. It would make no sense. Maximum freedom means freedom of thought and speech, of elections and of the press as well as freedom to own property.

These are known as civil liberties and are essential for any just society. These freedoms are so basic and important that they cannot be sacrificed to provide for a more equal distribution of wealth. Therefore it is the first responsibility of government to provide for a just society by guaranteeing equal civil liberties for all citizens. Since this would be the first choice of everyone's *best possible position*, Rawls claims it gives us the first principle of justice. 'First, each person is to have an equal right to the most extensive basic liberty compatible with a similar liberty for others' (520). From this principle come principles of equality. For example, it rules out discrimination, and the equality principle rules in the right to equal opportunity. So, for example, people who have equal ability and motivation should have equal chance of success no matter what their background.

Wealthiest Possible Position

Once civil liberties are provided for us, we will then want to choose the wealth we would like our position in society to have. Here again, guided by the rational choice of choosing *best possible position*, everyone would rationally choose the highest amount possible and this means there will be an equality of wealth with everyone getting the highest. Rawls says 'the sensible thing' would be to choose an equal distribution of wealth so you would not lose out (522). This choice both suits ourselves and ensures that no one does better than us by their choice when they pick their slip from the lottery drum. So, *best possible economic position* is what we will write on the lottery slip. Since everybody will write this on their slip, when we get to pick out a slip we will see that we all get positions of actual economic equality.

However, Rawls says there is no reason why this arrangement of actual equality should be final, provided it can be bettered. This leads him to the view that if, in practice, inequalities in positions give rise to an improvement in the circumstances of some people who otherwise would be worse off if those inequalities did not exist, then those inequalities are justified (522). Put simply in financial terms, if *best possible economic position* means €500 a week where everyone gets the same and it means €550 for the lowest position where there is inequality, with some getting €600 and others €650, etc., then inequality is justified because it has brought up the best possible position for those getting least.

In practice, Rawls argues, if 'various incentives' succeed in producing a wealthier society overall that improves the position of the least well-off while resulting in income inequality, then that inequality is justified (522). It is justified because it is something we would choose. We would see this as a rational choice to make. It is the choice that, in practice, will result in the *best possible economic position* for us no matter what slip we pick out of the lottery drum.

So, if I set up my own business and make a lot of money and by doing so employ staff and pay taxes, taxes that contribute to the well-being of others who do not benefit as much as me, then this is just because I have improved their starting position. When we all pick our slip we will be better off than we otherwise would have been because of this arrangement. Even if we pick the least position we cannot argue that we have lost out because the inequalities are justified only if they improve the least position from what it would be under equality. So, 'there is no injustice in the greater benefits earned by a few provided that the situation of persons not so fortunate is thereby improved' (516). From this line of reasoning, Rawls gets his second principle of justice.

This is that everyone should gain from the way positions in society are arranged. 'Second: social and economic inequalities are to be arranged so that they are both:

- reasonably expected to be to everyone's advantage, and
- attached to positions and offices open to all' (520).

His principle emphasises that 'while the distribution of wealth and income need not be equal, it must be to everyone's advantage, and at the same time, positions of authority and offices of command must be accessible to all' (520).

In effect, this means that economic and social policy should aim to do two things simultaneously: maximise the overall amount of wealth while making sure that the least well-off benefit as much as possible. The least well-off should be catered for as much as possible in a way that is consistent with having incentives to provide for the wealthiest society. So, if asked to decide what justice should be from behind the veil, we would choose maximising the advantage of the least advantaged because it is the rational choice. It ensures we get the best possible position for ourselves no matter what slip we pick. To choose otherwise would be to risk losing out, and this would be irrational.

His principle of justice does allow some people to have more than others, but only if the effect of some people having more results in the well-being of the least well-off being promoted. It is a principle that guarantees that even the most disadvantaged members will have a decent standard of living, i.e. the best they could reasonably expect.

RAWLS'S THEORY AND SOCIAL CARE

Rawls's theory claims to prove why we are morally obliged to have a society that is directed toward improving the living standards of the poor. The poor deserve to live in a society that is organised to improve their circumstances, not out of charity, but on the basis of principles of justice that are logical and rational. Since these principles constitute a rational understanding of what justice means, governments and other institutions must be guided by them in deciding social policy in relation to tax levels and welfare benefits and so on (523). Governments are morally obliged to provide adequate care services to ensure that the position of people in need of care is the best possible one they could reasonably expect. The veil ensures that if it turns out that we are born with autism or some other disability, we have chosen a society which will provide the best possible services for us. As such, his theory represents a strong argument that advocacy requests for improved care services should be met as a matter of justice.

His theory also helps us understand why all have a right to equal opportunity, and that conditions in society in which some people are held back by practical obstacles such as poverty or lack of facilities infringe their right.

NOZICK'S ENTITLEMENT VIEW OF SOCIAL JUSTICE

Introduction

Nozick's theory is a direct response to Rawls's theory, and one that comes to the opposite conclusion. He argues people are entitled to keep their wealth and have no moral obligation to share it with the less well-off. Anything you obtain voluntarily you are entitled to keep or do with it as you please – it is your entitlement.

Criticism of Justice Related to Distribution

Nozick criticises the use of the words 'distribution' and 'redistribution' of wealth in deciding what is just. He argues that in using such words we are already assuming that justice relates to having some arrangement for a more equal share of wealth, but there is no reason why justice should have to be about providing for this equality.

No Central Moral Authority

Nozick's main problem with the idea of distribution is that it implies that there is some central power in society *with the moral authority* to share out the wealth. The reality is that there is no power having such moral authority and never has been. He accepts, of course, that there is a democratically elected government, but he says it has no right to take people's wealth off them in tax to distribute to others. 'There is no *central* distribution, no person or group *entitled to* control all the resources, jointly deciding how they are to be doled out' (Nozick 2004: 527). This is because that wealth does not belong to the government, it belongs to the people who have it. Wealth will only belong to the government if people give it to them voluntarily. However, we are not given any choice; governments take money from citizens in tax by force of law.

If there is no body with the moral right to distribute wealth, it makes no sense to talk of redistribution as a way of rectifying unfairness. He says 'we are not in the position of children who have been given portions of pie by someone who now makes last-minute adjustments to rectify careless cutting' (527).

He says we would find it very unjust if the government decided to distribute our marriage partners to us. We would say they have no right to do that. People are not the property of government. On the other hand, a government does give itself the right to distribute money, money which does not belong to them, but belongs to the people from whom they take it. So, he says, there is no more a right to distribute resources than there is a right to distribute 'mates in a society in which people choose whom they shall marry' (527).

He does not say the government should take no tax at all. It is reasonable to take some tax to provide common services of benefit to everyone, e.g. infra-structure such as roads, policing and defence. His objection is the injustice of using tax to give direct transfers of money to the needy in welfare payments and free or subsidised services. Also, he is not saying that the aim of caring for the needy is necessarily wrong. All he is saying is that it is wrong to do so by 'robbing the rich to provide for the poor'.

Justice as Entitlement

For Nozick, justice is a matter of being entitled to what you have as long as you got it voluntarily. In this sense he refers to all the things you have as your 'holdings'. What you have, you are entitled to hold. There is 'justice of acquisition' (how we get what we have) and 'justice of transfer' (how people give to others). In both cases justice is solely a matter of 'voluntary exchange'. That is, once it happens without in any way forcing or deceiving others, it is just (528). Voluntary means of obtaining and transferring wealth, or 'holdings', include such common practices as:

- Pay in return for work.
- Profits from the sale of goods or services.
- Gifts, including inheritance.
- Return on investments.
- Prize winnings.

All such means are fair because they have come about either by the choices you make on your own behalf or the choice other people make for you on your behalf. This leads to his principle of justice as quoted below:

From each as they choose, to each as they are chosen.

Nozick 2004: 532

EXAMPLE

It is perfectly just for a top soccer player to get, say, €150,000 per week. He freely accepts this (not surprisingly!) in return for offering his skills. Nobody is forced to pay him that amount. His pay is made up of a free decision by his club, which in turn is based on free decisions by spectators to buy tickets to matches, by TV companies paying to televise them and by fans buying club merchandise. In the same way, a person who works for low pay freely accepts what is freely offered. This is fair, no matter how high or low a wage he gets.

(adapted from Nozick: 533)

In this way, the just state is the one we end up with as the outcome of the countless free decisions which all the different individuals in society are entitled to make.

The Justice of Making Rectification

As we said, if a person uses non-voluntary means to acquire his holdings, i.e. the person from whom s/he gets them has not agreed to their transfer to him/her, then s/he is not entitled to them. Such means include:

- Theft.
- Fraud.
- Breach of contract.
- Force.

Examples of this arise from history where, for example, blacks and Jews were forced to work against their will. Other examples include the Aborigines in Australia and the Native Americans in the US, who had their land taken from them by European settlers. Nozick accepts that if in the past people gained their present holdings by unjust means, then the justice of entitlement requires that they make amends where possible. There is a valid principle of reparation. It may not be possible to establish the extent, or the beneficiaries, of the injustice if it occurred in the distant past. In 1999, the German government agreed to pay compensation to descendants of Jews used as forced labour under the Nazis.

The Injustice of Patterned Theories

If the state imposes some overall *pattern* to the way people come to acquire and increase their wealth, it is unjust. Nozick sees Rawls's principle that wealth should be distributed to maximise the advantage of the least well-off as an example of an unjust pattern.

Interference in People's Lives

Nozick's main objection to patterns is that they are impositions that interfere with people's lives. The problem with principles of justice such as Rawls's is that they 'cannot be realised without continuous interference in people's lives' (534). In addition, he goes so far as to claim that interfering in people's lives by requiring them to pay tax for welfare needs amounts to forced labour and is 'a violation of people's rights' (535). In taking x hours of a person's earnings from him/her in tax in order to pay for the welfare of others, the government is, in effect, forcing him/her to work for somebody else's purpose. He argues that people would object if the government introduced a new law requiring them to work so many extra hours to pay for other people's welfare needs, but, in effect this is what is already happening because our earnings for a certain number of hours makes up the tax we pay that goes on welfare.

He goes even further. He claims that requiring us to work x hours to pay tax makes the government a 'part-owner' of us (537). It gives them a property right over us, and they are forcing us to behave as they want.

Non-voluntary Nature of Paying Tax for Social Care

Nozick's problem with paying tax to the government to provide for welfare is that it is not a free decision which we make. It would be fine if the government sought and obtained agreement from everyone to tax their earnings to pay for welfare – then it would be fair. But this has never been done. He says 'everyone above a certain level is forced to contribute to the needy' (537). He says we are not free to say to the government, 'Don't compel me to contribute to others and don't provide for me via this compulsory mechanism if I am in need' (537). We can't opt out. The government forces us comply with their wishes.

NOZICK'S THEORY OF JUSTICE AND SOCIAL CARE

His theory does not support the spending of public money to provide social care services. As he says, the minimal state is the only one that is justified, i.e. the state that does the least to help people directly (527). Therefore, the only way his theory could be considered to support social care is in its support for the view that the best way to care for people is to encourage them to be self-reliant. One of the values of social care is indeed to enable clients to have as much self-reliance as possible, but for many who need assistance, this cannot be achieved (or only after great hardship) without direct state help. What is more, many people needing care have little capacity to become self-reliant even with family support, such as older people and those with significant disabilities.

Note on Nozick's Modification of his View

Nozick softened his views in his later writings. He refers to a basic-level ethics of 'co-operation for mutual benefit' and a higher-level ethics of 'responsiveness and caring for others and positive aid'. He admitted in an interview that, while remaining a libertarian (one who values personal liberty highly), he was no longer 'as hardcore a libertarian as before' (see www.juliansanchez.com/nozick.html).

Exercise 11.1

Question for Consideration and Discussion: How Just is Irish Society?

In the light of the following information, consider the views of Aristotle, Rawls and Nozick on how Irish society is providing for social justice.

1. A Revenue Commissioners' report revealed that in 2002 there were forty-three people earning over €1 million who legally paid under 5 per cent tax, compared to the standard rate of 20 per cent and a higher rate of 42 per cent. This included six millionaires who paid no tax. The government defended the charge of providing tax breaks for the rich. It argued that the schemes encourage investment, which helps achieve economic and social objectives, notably to create jobs. From 2007, the government is phasing out seven property-based schemes on the basis that they are no longer needed. It expects, in time, that high earners will pay a minimum of 20 per cent. (Source: Liam Reed, Laura Slattery, *Irish Times*, 27 June 2006.)

2. *Measuring Ireland's Progress*, 2005, a Central Statistics Office report, revealed that Ireland had the lowest unemployment rate in the EU in 2005 at 4·2 per cent. However, Ireland spends less than other EU countries on social protection, i.e. on benefits and services which help people from becoming or remaining poor. In 2002, it was the lowest of the fifteen EU countries, and half the rate for Sweden. (Source: www.cso.ie/releasespublications/.)

CRITICAL EVALUATION

Aristotle's View

Aristotle's view of social justice is dependant on accepting his view of human nature as rational and social, and that practising virtues is the way to achieve human fulfilment. As we saw in considering Aristotle's ethics, this view is open to criticism. Rationality is not necessarily the defining feature of being human. At the same time, his view of social justice is one that is reasonable. For many who are concerned about injustices in society, and in the world, Aristotle has given a reasonable explanation of justice as a balance or fair share in living standards, and injustice as a big divide.

Rawls's View

Hypothetical Nature of Conditions for Deciding on Justice Principles

Rawls's veil condition for deciding on principles of justice is a version of the social contract, which we saw in Chapter 10. It is based on an agreement between all citizens on the kind of society they want. But the social contract is a purely hypothetical agreement. It never actually occurred or is ever likely to occur. Thus Rawls's theory can be criticised on the grounds that we do not know for sure what decision people would actually make if given the opportunity.

More than One Rational Choice

For Rawls's theory to work, he has to assume that all signatories to the contract see the rational choice as one in which they do not gamble. In other words, they see the rational choice as the safest one whereby they make sure they don't lose out in comparison to others. You could argue that another rational choice would be to choose the principle of the greatest happiness of the greatest number. It seems rational to choose a society based on trying to provide for the greatest happiness of the most people, even if this means some have to lose out and are not provided for as a priority. Kymlicka also makes this point (2004: 188).

Assumes People are Equal by Nature

Rawls's theory assumes people have a natural equality. This is the reason why he argues that the original position behind the veil is fair. Yet nowhere in his theory does he prove that people do have a natural equality. It's true that a natural equality of moral status between people accords with what most people see as central to any ethics. However, the only way of showing it to be true is to appeal to it as self-evident – and not everyone would agree that it is self-evident. Kymlicka makes this point also (2004: 188).

Reflective Equilibrium

You may have formed the view that Rawls's theory is highly implausible and unlikely to win agreement. After all, life is not like being in the original veil of ignorance condition, and it is too much to expect that we should be guided by our thoughts of it, especially as people have different ideas of justice. For utilitarians, justice is the greatest happiness principle, whereas for Nozick and his followers it is the principles of entitlement to what you have obtained voluntarily. However, Rawls proposed a method which, he believed, if people followed they would come to agree on principles consistent with his. In general and simple terms, he asks that we all look at the principles behind our differing ideas on justice in the light of the kinds of things those views of justice commit us to in practice. We then compare our principles and the things they imply with other people's to see which are the most rational. From this process of trying to get different principles and their associated meaning in practice to be consistent with each other, he believed people would find reason to adjust their principles. At the end of the process, a general understanding and agreement that one set of principles (his set) had more consistency or coherence than any other set would emerge.

However, he later changed his view on the likelihood of this agreement happening. He came to think that people would still stick to their views and that there would be diversity rather than consensus. Nevertheless, this process, called 'reflective equilibrium', is regarded by some as a useful *procedural* way of finding consistency and agreement on moral issues in general. In one form, called *narrow* reflective equilibrium, we try to see if our moral views are consistent with our principles. If they're not, then we need to adjust our views to make them more consistent with our principles – or else adjust our principles. For example, a question of consistency arises for a person who, on the basis of a right-to-life principle, is opposed to abortion from the stage of conception but who also holds the view that stem-cell research on embryos to find cures for diseases is morally acceptable. A similar question of consistency would arise if the same person supported a war (especially one in which there are likely to be fatalities among children and pregnant women) without that war being a morally just war. It is a matter of trying to reconcile our views in the light of our principles and, if we can't, of adjusting our views or else of adjusting our understanding of our principles to enable us to maintain our views.

In *wider* reflective equilibrium we test our views, and the principles that support them, against the understanding provided in different moral theories.

Nozick's View

Points Up a Legitimate Problem?

Nozick is not necessarily against the idea that it is morally good to provide social care. His point is merely that there is no justification for requiring people to pay for it in tax if they don't want to. It is not justice to require them to do so. Providing the money for care can only be a matter of individual choice – it is not a matter of justice. If he is right, it leaves a huge problem of how social services are to be provided because tax revenue is the main way of paying for it. However, it may be that if given the choice, most of us would agree to pay tax to provide care services. What do you think?

Supports Libertarianism

His view has been, and continues to be, influential in practice. This is because it supports the libertarian view that individual liberty is the most important value, in particular the liberty to earn and keep wealth without undue interference from government. In general terms, the libertarian approach supports (on moral grounds) policies of low tax on profits and earnings and low spending by government on social services.

Democracy Provides Government Moral Authority

The nature of democracy is the consent of the people to be governed in the best interests of *all* citizens, not just some. Therefore, it can be argued that this gives the government the moral authority, and obligation, to provide for the interests of those who have valid reasons for not being able to provide for their own needs.

People Are Not Free to the Same Extent

Nozick's theory depends on accepting the view that all actions people take are voluntary. Once they are, then nobody is wronged and justice prevails. However, people are not free to the same extent to make voluntary decisions. As we saw in Chapter 7, poverty restricts freedom of action and of choice. People born into poverty do not have, in practice, the same absence of restriction on them as people who are wealthy. Poverty, disability and old age limit people's choices. It is difficult, then, to see how they can be expected to acquire holdings as freely as people who are well-off. While they may be able to make a voluntary decision, they do not have the same scope in which to do so as others.

Underestimates Interdependence

Work is the main way in which people acquire their wealth, but work needs an environment in which everybody co-operates if it is to succeed. Large elements of this environment, such as providing healthy, educated citizens as well as security and infrastructure are provided by the state. You could argue, as a result, that people have obligations to the state over and above paying for services that directly benefit them, since the state pays for so much on which they depend if they are to become wealthy.

In addition, you can argue that everybody contributes toward society becoming prosperous. For example, the unemployed, disabled and older people perform social roles such as consumers, parents, carers, lovers and loved ones, all of which are either directly or indirectly related to making society prosperous. Nozick, you could argue, takes an unjustifiably narrow view of society made up of individuals as economic units who act in isolation from each other. A more accurate picture is one of a vast web of interdependency in which everyone contributes something to enable the system to work effectively in generating wealth.

REVIEW

Social justice is a key ethical requirement that underpins social care. A difficulty with it is that it can be understood in different ways, which indicate different levels of obligation to provide for those who need social care. For Aristotle and Rawls there is an obligation for social policy to be directed toward providing for the less well-off. Nozick is associated with the view that people are entitled to keep what they have acquired legitimately and not have to pay for the welfare of others beyond some minimum necessary level. Political parties support one position or the other in different degrees. Advocacy claims for social justice for those in need of care can be advanced based on an informed and critically evaluated understanding of how social justice can be understood.

FURTHER READING

Scally, J. (ed.) (2003) *A Just Society? Ethics and Values in Contemporary Ireland*, The Liffey Press.
Nozick, R. (1974) *Anarchy, State and Utopia*, Blackwell.
Rawls, J. (1971) *A Theory of Justice*, Oxford University Press.

REFERENCES

Aristotle (1955) *The Ethics of Aristotle, The Nicomachean Ethics*, Penguin Classics.
Kymlicka, W. (2004) 'The Social Contract Tradition' in *A Companion to Ethics*, P. Singer (ed.), Blackwell.
Mill, J. (1944) *Utilitarianism, Liberty and Representative Government*, Everyman's Library.
Nozick, R. (2004) 'The Entitlement Theory of Justice' in *Ethics in Practice: An Anthology*, 2nd ed., H. LaFollette (ed.), Blackwell.
Rawls, J. (2004) 'A Theory of Justice' in *Ethics in Practice: An Anthology*, 2nd ed., H. LaFollette (ed.), Blackwell.

12
Conclusion

We have seen that a number of values can be considered to inform, support and provide justification for social care. They provide bearings for dealing with casework, with providing for a more caring society and for developing an informed viewpoint on particular moral issues. They have been summed up as belonging to either one of two broad categories: detached and engaged (Gilligan cited in Banks 2004: 90). The more *detached* values relate to duty, the utilitarian greatest happiness principle, rights, social contracts and social justice. The more *engaged* values relate to well-being, respect and care, empathy, acceptance of difference and social well-being. The values in each category are relevant for guiding social care ethics in general. The relevance of one value more than another in practice will depend on the issue and its context. Both categories of values have traditionally been part of social work. They can be looked on as two sides of the same coin (Banks 2004: 93; 186–70).

We have also seen that the philosophical basis for these values is open to criticism. This is not to say that the criticisms are right and that they in some way disprove the values. It is to say that, as far as human understanding can grasp the basis for values, the basis can be contested.

Our engagement with values and with our ethical sensibility can be considered to have deep and powerful roots that cannot be clearly or fully understood. Iris Murdoch takes this view. For her, our sense of morality is what makes us 'uniquely human'. For example, it is our human moral sense that makes us want to help famine and disaster victims. It is why we condemn the torture of prisoners and demand that governments that allow it end the practice. It is what makes us think that for anyone to have to sleep rough in the streets is *not right*. Iris Murdoch believes it is as if our sense of ethics 'came to us from elsewhere'. She sees it as 'an intimation of something higher' (1992: 26).

This *something higher* is called a *transcendent* source. This means a sense of belonging to something larger than ourselves. For those who have a religious belief, the transcendent source is God. At the same time, she argues that whether a person takes their morals from their religious belief or from values without the backing of religious belief, there is still some ultimate guide at work (1992: 511). For Parekh, whose ideas we looked at in considering the value of acceptance of cultural difference, the transcendent is our membership of the human community from the partial perspective of our particular culture. We engage with the transcendent through a process of rational intercultural dialogue to try to find more understanding of human values (2000: 339).

For Iris Murdoch, the sense of the transcendent behind ethics is more mysterious. She sees evidence for it in art. She describes a work of art as like 'a picture of goodness itself' (1992: 9). How could this be? One way of trying to understand this is to see what the essential qualities of a work of art are, and then to see how they might also underlie our sense of ethics. Wolterstorff mentions three essential qualities. These are that the work provides a sense of unity of coherence or completeness, that it is internally rich, and that is intense or bright (1980: 164–8). These are general and rather vague qualities, but they ultimately underlie why we think a work of art is good. If what Iris Murdoch is suggesting is right, then when we look at, say, a great painting, we see in these qualities the essence of worth or value, the same worth or value that sustains a moral framework. Such moral frameworks, or what are called *value systems*, include any based on one (or a combination) of the values we have looked at, including the framework (now common) called *expressive individualism* within which the individual values his/her own self-realisation as the primary value. They also include the value systems of particular religions. Applying art qualities to ethics we can, I think, have some understanding that particular value frameworks which people come to have as their guides provide them with unity of coherence or completeness, along with a sense of having something internally rich and bright.

Works of art are many and various, yet retain the essential qualities of art. Moral frameworks, too, are many and various. This is particularly so when we consider that people find different ways of engaging with a framework. They endow certain features of their framework with particular worth and downplay or disregard others features. This is also the case with religious value systems. For example, some people are described as *liberal*, others as *orthodox*, and there are many shades in between. So, in the same way as there are many different artworks all providing the essential qualities of art, there is a diversity of moral frameworks or value systems, which overlap in some respects, all providing the same essential qualities of unity of coherence or completeness, internal richness and intensity or brightness. In this way, the moral frameworks can be seen to implement in behaviour the worth or value which we get from art. This way of looking at ethics has direct relevance for helping us to see value in other people's value systems and practices that are different to our own. It can help us to see richness in cultural and moral difference rather than opposition.

At a basic level we need values as reference points if we are to function in our personal and social lives. Without at least some framework we experience inconsistencies and fragmentation which make it difficult to cope by responding meaningfully to situations. At the level of art, this framework of value is made available in a distilled or concentrated form. Taylor speaks of how, from engaging with art, we can experience 'epiphanies' of fulfilment, however brief and fleeting they are, and of how we can sense in them no less than the very source of morality itself (1989: 425; 428; 431; 477).

A view of the moral source located in art can seem detached from life, but there is a practical, ordinary everyday side to it. This brings us back to an idea mentioned in Chapter 2 of ethics as the art of living. It is an idea associated in particular with Aristotle's ethics. Drawing on his ethics, Martha C. Nussbaum (1990) has explored the understanding of ethics as a practical art through looking at how well (or badly) characters in novels manage the opportunities, challenges and setbacks in the very particular circumstances of their lives, having regard to their human nature and forces outside their control. Aristotle's aim for ethical action is that, under the guidance of the virtues, we try to achieve balance (*symmetry* or *harmony* in art terms) in the effect our response has on any situation, taking into account our own needs and desires for well-being, the needs and desires of others and society in general. To practise ethics as an art does not mean acquiring the mannerisms of an artist, however we might imagine them, nor does it mean living according to some preconceived notion of balance or harmony and trying to apply it. It means first and foremost being open to a situation as fully as possible in order to have an adequate response. It requires us to develop awareness and sensitivity in the hope of bringing about an outcome that is right and fitting.

REFERENCES

Banks, S. (2004) *Ethics, Accountability and the Social Professions*, Palgrave Macmillan.

Murdoch, I. (1992) *Metaphysics as a Guide to Morals*, Chatto & Windus.

Nussbaum, M. (1990) *Love's Knowledge: Essays on Philosophy and Literature*, Oxford University Press.

Parekh, B. (2000) *Rethinking Multiculturalism: Cultural Diversity and Political Theory*, Palgrave Macmillan.

Taylor, C. (1989) *Sources of the Self: The Making of the Modern Identity*, Cambridge University Press.

Wolterstorff, N. (1980) *Art in Action: Towards a Christian Aesthetic*, William B. Eerdmans Publishing Company.

Index